The Potato: Its History and Culture
With a Descriptive List of Heirloom Potato Varieties

by Archibald Findlay

with an introduction by Roger Chambers

This work contains material that was originally published in 1905.

This publication was created and published for the public benefit, utilizing public funding and is within the Public Domain.

This edition is reprinted for educational purposes and in accordance with all applicable Federal Laws.

Introduction Copyright 2018 by Roger Chambers

COVER CREDITS

Front Cover
Potatoes texture Clue169 by 16:9clue
[CC BY 2.0 - http://creativecommons.org/licenses/by/2.0],
via Wikimedia Commons

Back Cover
From interior

Research / Sources
Wikimedia Commons
www.Commons.Wikimedia.org

Many thanks to all the incredible photographers, artists,
researchers, and archivists who share their great work.

PLEASE NOTE :
As with all reprinted books of this age that are intended to perfectly reproduce the original edition, considerable pains and effort had to be undertaken to correct fading and sometimes outright damage to existing proofs of this title. At times, this task can be quite monumental, requiring an almost total rebuilding of some pages from digital proofs of multiple copies. Despite this, imperfections still sometimes exist in the final proof and may detract slightly from the visual appearance of the text.

DISCLAIMER :
Due to the age of this book, some methods or practices may have been deemed unsafe or unacceptable in the interim years. In utilizing the information herein, you do so at your own risk. We republish antiquarian books without judgment or revisionism, solely for their historical and cultural importance, and for educational purposes.

Self Reliance Books

Get more historic titles on animal and stock breeding, gardening and old fashioned skills by visiting us at:

http://selfreliancebooks.blogspot.com/

introduction

I am very pleased to present to you another wonderful old book on horticulture – *The Potato : Its History and Culture* . It was written by Archibald Findlay, and first published in 1905, making it well over a century old.

These days, many of us have concerns about our broken food system – drugs and chemicals in our food, GMOs, artificial sweeteners and other synthetic, lab-made additives, etc.

Here at **Self-Reliance Books** we strive to help you mitigate these problems by bringing you the best in *dusty-old-book-knowledge* to aid you in your quest for a more independent and self-sufficient way of life.

The book covers topics including *The Potato : Its History and Culture, The Potato and Some of Its Near Relatives, Cultivation of the Potato, Manuring, Seeding, How New Varieties of Potatoes and Produced,* and more.

A wonderful old book on the humble Potato, and a great addition to the libraries of all those who grow potatoes as a crop, or anybody considering taking the plunge.

~ *Roger Chambers*
State of Jefferson, January 2018

From Chalk Drawing by F. Findlay.

Yours truly,
N. Findlay

PREFACE.

AFTER a few more years of work and gathered knowledge, I again beg to submit the result of my experience to the indulgent reader in the following pages.

I have tried to set forth in few words, and in the plainest language at my command—studiously avoiding those matters that are only of importance to the few, but keeping always in view the things that are of importance to what I may call the great potato world, the British Farmer, the Market Gardener, the Suburban Grower, and the Rural Cottager—what I deem to be of more than passing interest for them to know in the management of this important crop, a crop which, I think, few will care to dispute is of the very first importance, not only to those I have specially mentioned, but to the teeming millions of all ranks and conditions. If I have succeeded so far, as I wish and hope, I have succeeded in my highest ambition.

In the illustrations I have tried to convey an idea of the extent of the business that has grown round my endeavour to improve the potato, and, as far as a picture can give it, the appearance of the potatoes I have given to the world. In addition, I have attempted to depict some of my surroundings and interests apart from the potato—my interest in farm animals, and the efforts I have made for the better housing of my work-people.

I would here apologise for the delay that has taken place in the issue of this work, but, on the whole, I do not think the delay is altogether to be regretted, as I have thus been enabled to enlarge the scope of the book very much beyond my original intention.

A. F.

CONTENTS.

	PAGE
The Potato: Its History and Culture	1
The Potato and some of its near Relations	3
Cultivation of the Potato—	
The Soil and its Preparation	3
Manuring	4
A New Disease in Potatoes	6
Seeding	8
Cultivation	10
Harvesting and Storing	11
The Development of New Breeds of Potatoes	14
How New Varieties of Potatoes are Produced	23

APPENDIX.

The Potato Up-to-Date	28
A Day with Findlay at Markinch	33
Potato Growing in Scotland	35
Important Inspection of Potatoes in Fife	36
Exhibition of Mr Findlay's Potatoes at Markinch	37
Exhibition of Potatoes at Markinch	39
New Markinch Potatoes	41
Practice with Science: Potato Propagation in Fifeshire	44
Potato Propagation	46
New Varieties of Potatoes	46
A Great Field Day at Markinch	47
Disease-Resisting Potatoes	50
Some Facts on Potato Growing	52
The Bruce and its Rivals	53
Interesting Exhibition of Potatoes at Markinch	55
Whole *versus* Cut Seed Potatoes	57
Potato Propagation	58
Presentation to the Raiser of the Bruce Potato	60
Potato Culture in Fife	64

DESCRIPTIVE LIST OF POTATOES.

	PAGE		PAGE
Findlay's Up-to-Date	67	Findlay's Aurora	70
Findlay's Farmer's Glory	67	Findlay's Conquest	70
Findlay's Goodhope	68	Findlay's Exhibition	71
Findlay's Lady Rosabelle	68	Findlay's Jeanie Deans	71
Findlay's British Queen	68	Findlay's Early Beauty	71
Findlay's Ruby Queen	69	Findlay's Lady Fife	72
Findlay's Snowdrift	69	Findlay's Lady Frances	72
Findlay's Eightyfold	69	Findlay's Her Majesty	72
Findlay's Pink-Eyed Russet	70	Findlay's The Bruce	73
Findlay's Challenge	70		

LATEST INTRODUCTIONS.

	PAGE		PAGE
Findlay's Langholme Model	76	Findlay's Colonist	79
Findlay's Mairsland Queen	76	Findlay's Evergood	79
Findlay's Gold Reef	76	Findlay's Mr Ambrose	80
Findlay's Diamond Reef	77	Findlay's Hibernia	80
Findlay's Million Maker	77	Findlay's Empress Queen	80
Findlay's Eldorado	77	Findlay's Queen of the Veldt	31
Findlay's Great Scot	78	Findlay's Klondyke	81
Findlay's Northern Star	78	Findlay's British Queen, No. 2	81
Findlay's Royal Kidney	78	Findlay's Up-to-Date, No. 2	82
Findlay's Goodfellow	79	Findlay's Empire Kidney	82

A Visit to Mr Findlay at Langholme ... 83
Mr Findlay in Lincolnshire ... 86

FINDLAY'S "QUEEN OF THE VELDT."

FINDLAY'S "CONQUEST."

Dressing and Dispatching Potatoes from Pits.

Workmen's Cottages, "Mairsland."

LIST OF ILLUSTRATIONS.

1.	Portrait	...	Frontispiece
2.	Glenglasserts, Mairsland	Facing page	1
3.	Howe o' Fife from Mairsland	On reverse	
4.	Findlay's Seed Warehouse, Auchtermuchty	Facing page	4
5.	Field of Eldorado and Ninety-five New Varieties	,,	5
6.	Findlay's Seed Warehouse (interior)	,,	8
7.	Findlay's Seed Warehouse (interior), showing Potatoes in Boxes	,,	9
8.	Bullock bred on Mairsland	,,	12
9.	Mairsland House and Steading from the North	,,	13
10.	Langholme House from Lawn	,,	16
11.	Langholme House from Public Road	,,	17
12.	Langholme Homestead from Public Road	,,	17
13.	Carts for Langholme	,,	20
14.	Ready to Start	,,	21
15.	Dressing and Dispatching Potatoes from Pits	,,	24
16.	Workmen's Cottages at Mairsland	,,	24
17.	Findlay's Queen of the Veldt	,,	25
18.	Findlay's Conquest	,,	25
19.	Cup presented to National Potato Society by Messrs Carter & Co., London, and Mr Findlay	,,	28
20.	Findlay's British Queen II.	,,	29
21.	Findlay's Million Maker	,,	29
22.	Findlay's Mairsland Queen in Boxes for Springing	,,	32
23.	Findlay's Million Maker in Boxes for Springing	,,	32
24.	Findlay's Gold Reef in Boxes for Springing	,,	33
25.	Findlay's Diamond Reef in Boxes for Springing	,,	33
26.	Mairsland House	,,	40
27.	Plot of Northern Star	,,	40
28.	Plot of Great Scot	,,	41
29.	Plot of Diamond Reef	,,	41
30.	Findlay's Diamond Reef	,,	44
31.	Findlay's Gold Reef	,,	44
32.	Findlay's Million Maker	,,	45
33.	Findlay's Great Scot	,,	45
34.	Plot of Million Maker	,,	48
35.	Plot of Eldorado	,,	48
36.	Plot of Un-named Hybrid Seedlings	,,	49

LIST OF ILLUSTRATIONS—Continued.

37.	Plot of Empire Kidney	Facing page	49
38.	Findlay's Farmer's Glory	,,	52
39.	Findlay's The Bruce	,,	52
40.	Findlay's Langholme Model	,,	53
41.	Findlay's Empire Kidney	,,	53
42.	Digging Findlay's Challenge	,,	56
43.	Findlay's Lady Fife	,,	60
44.	Findlay's Ruby Queen	,,	61
45.	Findlay's Snowdrift	,,	64
46.	Findlay's Early Beauty	,,	65
47.	Findlay's Her Majesty	,,	68
48.	Findlay's Jeanie Deans	,,	69
49.	Findlay's Lady Frances	,,	72
50.	View of Markinch	Facing advertisements	—

With the exception of Nos. 42 to 47 inclusive, the illustrations are by Mr F. Findlay from blocks prepared by the British Photo-Engraving Co., Coventry.

THE POTATO:

ITS HISTORY AND CULTURE.

WHEN the Spaniards under Pizarro invaded the Pacific slope of South America in 1535 they found the cultivation of the potato, under the beneficent rule of the Incas, a matter of ancient usage, in the temperate regions extending from Chile in the south to New Granada in the north, at altitudes varying with the latitude. The Spaniards soon discovered its merits, and sent it, no doubt, home to Spain as one of the treasures of their new empire, thus introducing it into Europe about 1560, at least some years before Sir Walter Raleigh and Thomas Herriott brought it to England—we might rather say to Ireland—for, so far as we can learn, it was on Sir Walter's Irish estate at Youghal it was first grown, and was described by Thomas Herriott, his companion, as the Virginian potato. For what reason it is difficult to understand, except we bear in mind that their ostensible voyage was to Virginia, and in the homeward voyage had, as was the fashion of the times, seized some Spanish ship returning from South America, and found some potatoes on board, for at that time it is hardly possible to believe it was in cultivation in any part of North America, at least on the east coast of that vast continent. I have often wondered how it got the name of potato, and I daresay so have all who have made its history a subject of enquiry, as its name in its own country is apenawk. From Herriott's description of the plant there is no doubt that it was the potato, and not the batata (the sweet potato), which at that time was often confounded with it.

There is also another matter—not of much importance beyond showing there was a possibility of some of the early English colonists in Virginia having got hold of the potato from Spanish or other traders or travellers, who had been to Chile or Peru either during the time of or after the Conquest; for Gerard tells us in his "Herbal," published in 1597, that he received from Virginia the potato, which he cultivated in his garden, and which agrees in all points with the potato as we know it; and as showing the esteem in which he held it, he is represented in his portrait at the beginning of the work holding a flowering branch of the plant in his hand. All the same, it is hardly possible for the potato to have been introduced into Virginia in Raleigh's time (1585), unless the ancient Mexicans had cultivated it, and that it had got spread about amongst the aborigines north of Mexico. According to De

A

Candolle, in his "Origin of Cultivated Plants," Dr Roulin, who had carefully studied the works on North America, says he finds no trace of the potato until after the arrival of Europeans. He also adds, on the authority of Dr Asa Gray, that Mr Harris, an authority on the language and customs of the North American tribes, was of the same opinion.

But be all these things as they may, it was in the manner we have described that it found its way into southern Europe, and how a little later on this great food plant was introduced by Sir Walter Raleigh and his companion Thomas Herriott into Britain sometime between the years 1585 and 1586. Some will have it that Sir Walter's companion, Thomas Herriott, was the party who introduced it; but I think that rests wholly on his having left a written description, as already mentioned, of the plant, which description is quoted by Sir Joseph Banks in "The Transactions of the Horticultural Society," 1805, vol. I. All the same, it must, in justice to Herriott, be said he was as fully interested in its cultivation as Sir Walter, if not more so. However, it was Sir Walter who demonstrated on his Irish estates its great value as a food plant, and, although a native of the southern hemisphere, that it could be successfully grown in the British Isles. Notwithstanding its many claims on popular attention, it met the common fate of nearly all that is good—if that good runs counter to the strong conservative instinct of the average Briton. Vulgar and learned prejudice metaphorically rose in arms against it; the layman wrote against it; the priest thundered at it from the pulpit as a dangerous thing of a dangerous race—a thing to be avoided by saint and sinner alike; and it is not until 219 years (1805) from the date of its introduction into Britain that we find Dr Buchan, in the 19th edition of his "Domestic Medicine," speaking of the potato as being only grown in Ireland and the north of England to any extent, and strongly urging its claims on all classes as a food-producing plant, as a means of preventing a recurrence of famine in the land.

It may not be out of place here to bring before the reader that in the end of the 18th and beginning of the 19th century there was a series of bad years, in which the British corn crops were practically destroyed, and a state bordering on famine prevailed. I am even led to believe that in remote and out-of-the-way places many died in these years of starvation. These were the conditions of the country, fresh in the memory if not actually prevailing, that made this philanthropic and learned doctor to urge the claims of the potato to more general cultivation. In support of his pleading, this enlightened writer quotes a letter from Sir John Methven to Sir William Pulteney. This letter bears the date of 4th April, 1801, and contains an account of Sir John's experience of getting his cottager to cultivate the potato on his fallow land. Notwithstanding all these endeavours—and I doubt not many other equally enlightened gentlemen urging its claims as a necessity of the times—the potato made slow progress in public favour; but like everything with solid merit, although compelled to wait, its day of popularity came, and we are told that, before it became a common farm crop, the ploughman lads, when offered a boiled egg or a boiled potato to finish off their mid-day meal with, invariably preferred the latter.

THE POTATO AND SOME OF ITS NEAR RELATIONS.

I think I might as well pause here, before proceeding with my ideas as how best to cultivate and preserve the potato from its many enemies, and make a few incidental remarks on the potato and some of it near relations.

The potato, the *Solanum tuberosum* of the botanist, after being long a matter of doubt and much debate, is now known to be a native of that part of South America known as Chile, and, from all evidence gathered, it is now plain that the plant can only be found in a really wild state in the rather cold regions of the plateaux of the Andes mountains of this part of South America. Now with this fact of native locale kept steadily before you, I think you will understand the great cause of the prominence of Scotland, more especially the hilly and colder parts, as the proper regions from which to have seed from for those growing potatoes on more southern lands, or land anywhere near sea level. The other tuber-bearing members of this order of plants are the *Solanum comanersonii* of Dunal; *Solanum Maglia* of Molina, also a native of Chile; *Solanum immite*, a native of Peru; and *Solanum verrucosum*, a native of Mexico, and some others of less importance. I may here mention that none of these or the other tuber-bearing solanums have been found to be of any commercial value, notwithstanding the efforts of many cultivators—although I lately saw a letter from an American house offering one of the above as one of the grandest tuber-bearing plants in existence, and sure to beat everything; but I am afraid that, notwithstanding its several shortcomings, a really good substitute (leaving the something better out of our consideration) is yet a long way off, and that our best safety lies in giving this noble plant (the potato) our best attention in the matter of its development on the lines of *disease-resisting power, productiveness,* and *quality.*

CULTIVATION OF THE POTATO.

THE SOIL AND ITS PREPARATION.

That the potato will grow on almost any kind of soil is a fact I think known to the merest novice in matters agricultural. But at the same time, I am of opinion that it is about the greatest waste of energy imaginable to make the attempt to do so profitably on what are known as heavy lands. In other words, it is only on what are known as free and light soils that this can be done, and only if these are naturally or artificially well drained. For my own part, I prefer sandy, or it may be gravelly soil. No doubt many object to such soils, by reason of some varieties of potatoes when grown on them having a tendency to be what is termed "sprainged" in some parts of Scotland, and in some parts of England "cankered," *i.e.*, in having brown markings in the flesh of the tuber, which turn black and hard on being cooked, when grown on this class of soil. But this can be very much if not altogether prevented by a liberal allowance of potash and other alkaline constituents in the manure used in the growing of this crop. Many cultivators I have come in contact with, judging by their methods, seem to be of opinion that the potato is a surface-rooting plant, and that if the soil is well loosened by tilling and grubbing to the depth of six or eight inches, the requirements of the plant have been met in that direction; but the result of my experience in my experimental plots, and so also of my observation, wherever deep cultivation has been systematically gone about, is that the potato plant yields out of all proportion to the outlay where deep cultivation is practised. But at the same time, the reader must bear in mind that I am not advocating deep cultivation in the sense of burying the true soil and bringing up to the surface a poor, often obnoxious, subsoil. What I recommend is subsoiling, and that as often at least as potatoes are grown on the same land, and that as deeply as possible.

And to those who are sceptical as to the benefits to be derived from this practice, I would advise them to try an acre so treated of their potato break, otherwise treating that part as the other portions of the same field, and test this part by weighing the produce as against an equal portion of the same field when the crop has reached maturity. I will not occupy time and space by going into the many scientific reasons that might be adduced in support of this method of culture—such as the deeper aeration, and consequent nitrification of the soil. The wider field thus formed from which the plant can draw its food, the greater power to resist drought in a dry season, and a greater absorbent power in a wet one, I think all these and many more reasons will be present in the mind of the ordinary reader of our current agricultural intelligence, and induce him to give a fair trial to what, I am persuaded, will be a leading feature in the agriculture of the future, and in the matter of potato culture of the first importance.

Then let us suppose this deep cultivation has been accomplished in the autumn or early winter. The next thing of supreme importance—for bear in mind the object we have now in view is to have everything in such order that the potato plant shall have the least possible drawbacks or obstacles to encounter in the fullest possible development of tubers—is to have the land thoroughly pulverised and cleaned in the early spring of knot and couch grass. I may here remark, that for cleaning land of coltsfoot, thistles, and other deep-rooting weeds that are so common, I know of nothing so efficacious as this deep tillage and subsoiling I have been recommending; and although that was the only good to be attained by its practice, it would be profitable to adopt on much of our arable lands. The cleaning of the land of the grass and other weed roots should be particularly attended to, especially if the varieties to be grown are early ones, as these, though rapid in growth, are generally so deficient in top as to offer no check to the growth of the weeds. This particular care in cleaning is not so imperative where late and strong-growing varieties, such as Up-to-Date and Northern Star, are to be grown under liberal manurial treatment. I have repeatedly cleaned some very foul land by growing close, full crops of Up-to-Date and other strong-growing varieties.

MANURING.

As we all understand, we cannot get along with this crop without dealing with the question of muck *v.* manure. But in the present case, to meet the prevailing prejudice in favour of muck for this crop, I will adopt a middle course—though notwithstanding differing all the while—as my experience is that the best potatoes in every respect can be grown with chemical manures alone. To avoid repeating myself here you will find on pages further on my reasons fully stated for this preference, and an account of benefits of no mean importance that seem to follow. Let us now suppose the land to be dealt with is of the light sandy nature to which I have referred, and in low manurial condition; then I say give it not less than ten to fifteen loads of good farmyard manure to the statute acre before commencing to cultivate, and early in January sow broadcast over the land not less than 4 cwt. of kainit to the statute acre, and 3 cwt. of high-class superphosphates. If the land shows any tillyness or moss in the subsoil use basic slag or ground lime at the rate of say 10 cwt. per acre. And immediately before planting, sow broadcast *over* the drills sulphate of ammonia at the rate of 1½ cwt. per acre. This manurial treatment will grow a bumper crop in an ordinary season.

It may not be out of place here to place before you a few facts in relation to the growing of potatoes with purely artificial manures. In the first place, let us have a look in to see what the potato is made up of, and, from our observation, come to a conclusion as to its food requirements. Speaking broadly, the potato is composed of starch, gluten, and woody fibre. The starch, which is the larger part, as is well known is a form of carbon, and is wholly taken from the atmosphere; and they had it on the authority of the late John Wilson, professor of agriculture in the University of Edinburgh, that an 8-ton crop of potatoes per acre removed from the soil in which they were grown—of the bases or alkaline earths, 90 lbs. potash, 8 lbs. soda, 5 lbs. lime, 7 lbs. magnesia; and of the acids, 34 lbs. sulphuric acid, 10 lbs. phosphoric acid, 10 lbs. hydrochloric acid—in all, 174 lbs. of inorganic matter. And that was for tubers alone: if we allow an equal quantity for the tops, that brought the quantity up to about 358 lbs. of inorganic matter to an 8-ton crop. Now, as we increase the crop to ten, twelve, or sixteen tons, so do we increase the drain on these inorganic substances. And you will understand that if any of us fail to keep up this supply of inorganic plant food, and in an available form. the land will become potato sick. In other words, there is no food, or only such a meagre supply, that the plants become sickly, and fall ready victims to every form of disease. As is well known, I often grow the same variety of potatoes on the same land for several years in succession, yet, strange to say, instead of my potatoes falling off year by year as one might expect, my last crop is very often the best; but my practice is, so far as I can calculate, to apply 100 lbs. of these inorganic substances per acre beyond the requirements of each crop.

Now the next matter for our consideration is, how are we to supply these in suitable form with the least outlay of money. We shall suppose that the land on which we are proposing to grow potatoes is of a light and suitable nature for this crop. I would advise the land being tilled early as possible in the winter, and immediately thereafter sow broadcast over it 6 cwts. kainit per acre, which will supply the necessary quantity of potash, soda, and hydrochloric acid. At the same time, or shortly thereafter, sow in the same manner an equal quantity of 28 per cent. superphosphate of lime, which will supply the necessary quantity of phosphoric acid as well as lime. In growing *very early potatoes* with this manurial preparation, I prefer sowing in the drill, before the potatoes have been put down, nitrate of soda at the rate of 1 cwt. per acre. Before moulding up in the summer, if the crop seems to want it, apply ½ to ¾ cwt. of nitrate of soda; but in this matter the grower must be guided by the appearance of his crop. With mid-season and late varieties apply 1 cwt. sulphate of ammonia in preference to nitrate of soda just before putting down the sets; and at moulding time in the summer apply an equal quantity of ammonia sulphate—I mean 1 cwt. With this very cheap manure I have grown some wonderful crops of potatoes, of beautiful, steady growth, full of vigour and health, yet on land that was manurially about as poor as it could be; the next crop better; the following more vigorous still; while the corn and grass that followed were extra crops—although this land bore the character of being perfectly unfit to bear either corn or grass. But all the same, there are advantages to be derived from the use of farmyard manure that must never be lost sight of by the cultivator of the land, such is its tendency to make heavy lands freer; and further, being wholly decaying vegetable matter, the humus derived therefrom is of first importance as a general ameliator of the soil, no matter whether light or heavy. I am inclined to counsel a well-balanced use of both on the lines of the food requirements of the plants you grow or intend to grow.

A NEW DISEASE IN POTATOES.

I may here I think with advantage introduce the substance of an article I wrote by request for the Intelligence Department of the Board of Agriculture in 1894. Owing to extreme climatic conditions, "spraing" was a very common fault in the crop of 1893—so common, in fact, on lands where formerly, if it ever appeared at all, only in such a trifling way as not to arrest attention; but this season it was so common on all lands of a light nature as to be spoken of as a new disease of a most insidious kind, as there was no indication of anything being wrong until you had cut the tuber. So having had a fair look round and a careful examination of the crops in my own neighbourhood, and enquiring outside of this, I came to the only conclusion possible, that it was only the potato grower's old acquaintance—no doubt very much accentuated by reason of extreme climatic conditions prevailing during the summer and autumn—in some parts of Scotland called "sprain," in other parts of Scotland "spraing," which, according to Dr Jamieson, means a long stripe, including the idea of variegation. "Sprainging," according to the same authority, means tints or shades of colour; now, that exactly describes what we have here, for on cutting a potato with this fault, you find it variegated in the sense that it is marked in a lesser or greater degree with stripes and spots of various shades of brown—some of them so faint as scarcely to be visible, and others so dark as almost to be black—which, with the white setting of the unaffected parts, conveys a sense of true variegation. In some parts of England it is spoken of as "canker," but I prefer the Scotch name "spraing" (possibly on account of nationality) as best describing this fault in the potato. So much for the name of this so-called disease.

I shall now consider in the light of my experience the varieties in which this fault or peculiarity is most common, and their special features. I have never found it in very early varieties, or in the more forward of the second early class of potatoes. I have, however, attributed their immunity in a great measure to the fact that they finish their growth under better weather conditions than the later varieties. But with the later second earlies, and maincrop, or late varieties, it has always been a common fault in this district of Fife, especially in that *firm, dry* order of potato originally represented here, in my time, by Paterson's Victoria and its direct descendant the Champion, and now by Clark's Maincrop Kidney. I might have said by the Fluke, for I understand the Victoria was a *natural* seedling from the Fluke, as the Champion and Maincrop Kidney are from the Victoria. I have even found hybrids from the Victoria, such as my own Thane of Fife, particularly liable to this fault, and liable in proportion as they seemed to take after that variety; and the same remarks apply to hybrids sent out by other growers in which the Fluke and Victoria blood—if I may use the term—is a leading feature.

Yet you must not understand me to mean that "spraing" is a constant feature even in these varieties, but only that they show a distinct liability to "spraing" when grown under certain conditions. On clay land, or loam lying on clay or on sharp, clean gravel, or on sharp, clean gravelly soil, I have never seen it; but it is almost constant in these varieties when grown on sandy loam lying on soft, pale sand, or on sand in which there is ochre. In proportion to the amount of ochre in this class of soil have I found the proportion of "sprainged" tubers, which seems to me to point to mal-nutrition as being an important factor in the production of this unpleasant feature in these potatoes.

And I may here relate a set of circumstances that go far to convince me that the providing of a complete manure or food for the potato plant goes far to prevent "spraing" even in soil liable to produce it, and that an incomplete or one-sided manure—that is, a manure applied without consideration of the chemical condition of the soil and requirements of the plant—will produce "spraing"—I mean on the class of soil of which I have spoken as having a tendency to produce it.

Some years ago I rented for potato-growing purposes a piece of land that was notorious for this fault. The true soil was of very inferior quality and thin; the subsoil soft sand, showing *by bulk* or precipitation about 15 per cent. of ochry matter in its composition. It was soil on which nothing seemed to thrive excepting "yarr" and sorrel. After examination and consideration of its natural defects and character, I resolved to apply best kainit at the rate of 4 cwt. per statute acre, which I did early in the spring, and at time of planting gave a compound (chemical) manure at the rate of 10 cwt. per acre of the following values:— Ammonia, 5 per cent.; phosphates, 12 per cent. soluble, 8 per cent. insoluble; and potash, 12 per cent.—and had a very large crop of The Bruce, and no "spraing." Three years later I grew six or eight different kinds of potatoes, including The Thane—of which I have already spoken of as being liable to this fault—on the same piece of land, with the same manurial treatment. Result, a very full crop, and no "spraing." On the following year I again grew the same varieties on the same piece of land with precisely the same manurial treatment. I think the crop was the best I ever had, and again entirely free from "spraing." And I may here tell you of further benefits that have accrued through this treatment. After the potatoes it was sown with rye and grass and clover seeds. The rye was as fine a crop as one could wish to see; and the clover the finest to be seen anywhere in Fife, and not one plant of sorrel could be found in the whole plot; yet in a field adjoining, under the management of another, and differently treated (manurially), the potato crop was, though a full one, comparatively useless by reason of their being so badly "sprainged." And I may remark that this field had the advantage of lying in pasture for a considerable number of years previous to the potato crop.

My friend, Mr Lawson of Carriston, had a field of land of a very sandy nature, and from its character very likely to "spraing" potatoes. It had also lain for a number of years as pasture, had been fed upon, and had a heavy turf. He acted upon my suggestion as to manurial treatment, and he tells me that although he grew The Bruce, Her Majesty, Abundance, and Maincrop Kidney, that he does not think he has one "sprainged" potato; and I may add that I grew in 1893 over one hundred varieties under all possible conditions of soil, and I have not found amongst them one potato so affected, although I have used the knife freely wherever I thought I would find it.

And as a further illustration of my contention that this so-called "new disease" is, even in those varieties noted as being particularly prone to be affected, altogether a matter of soil and manurial treatment, I lately met in the Corn Exchange, Edinburgh, a well-known and extensive farmer who had suffered very much from it, and was very much impressed that potato growers had got to contend with a very obscure and insidious disease in their crops; for, as he said, it seemed to affect in a greater degree what they had always considered their hardiest varieties, giving as evidence that his Maincrop Kidneys, which never previously shown any appearance of blight, had turned out the worst.

I asked him on what kind of soil he grew them. "Well," he said, "parts of the field were light (sandy) and other parts of a heavier and damper (moister) nature, yet, strange to say," he continued, "they" (meaning the potatoes) "were worst on the fine dry soil, and none at all affected on the damper and harder land, which is the very opposite of what used to be with the old disease" (meaning the blight or disease caused by *peronaspora infestans*).

I then asked him how he manured his potatoes. "Never less than sixteen loads of *prime* farmyard manure to the statute acre, 5 cwt. of potato compound, and 1½ cwt. nitrate of soda when earthing up." I then asked him if the whole field received the same treatment, notwithstanding the visible and known differences of soil in it, and his answer was—"It all got the same treatment." And on my asking him if he did not think there was too much of the stimulating and forcing element in this treatment, his reply was— "That is what we always give."

Now this is only one account of a hundred of a similar kind I have had to listen to.

I have never had time, since asked to furnish the paper to the Board of Agriculture, to make a thorough study of the "sprainged" parts of the tuber under the microscope; but so far as I have. I can find no trace of *peronaspora infestans*, or any other *fungi;* but, if I am not mistaken, there is considerable compression and consequent rupture of the cell-walls; with thickening and discoloration of the same in the immediate neighbourhood and spreading outwards, which gives to the affected parts the appearance of shading off visible to the naked eye.

SEEDING.

I am very much afraid my readers, however much they may agree with me in theory after perusal, have in the past—judging from what I know is done all over the country— carried on a very different practice from what I am about to recommend. I have correspondents writing me from all the potato growing districts of Britain and Ireland for potatoes *seed size*. And when I ask them what I am to understand by this, the invariable answer is, "under 1¾-inch and over 1¼-inch riddle or sieve." Now, if there is a weedy, wasterful plant or ill-conditioned sport in the whole field or plot, it is in this class or size that its produce is sure to be found. Yet have commercial growers, and, if I am not much mistaken, most seed growers as well, been going on time out of mind using this class of tuber for seed, and so doing their best to ruin the best and hardiest varieties, deliberately shutting their eyes to all the evidence of nature and common-sense. And all the while they are looking wise and talking at large and learnedly over the rapid decadence of esteemed and popular varieties. I often wonder what would be said of the agriculturist who only used his light grain for seed, or bred his stock from the weeds and wasters of his flocks and herds. I may be told it is different with the potato, it being only an aggregation of underground buds. But having experimented in all directions, and having induced a few others to follow my methods, with identical results, I have come to the conclusion that the laws of reproduction find no exception in the potato, though what we use for and call seed is not a seed in the strict acceptance of the term, but, as I have already said, an aggregation of underground buds. And the practical outcome of the experiments of which I have been speaking clearly point out that the best and most profitable size of potato for seed purposes is from 3 to 3½ ounces in weight, which is about the size of a good hen's egg. or under a 2-inch and over a 1½-inch riddle or sieve, and planted whole or cut into not more than two sets. and about 15 or 18 inches apart in the drill; and the drills should be from 24 to 28 inches apart, the distance between the plants and between the drills being determined by the varieties having a moderate or heavy top. I may here remark that potatoes such as Northern Star seem to resent being grown in a crowded manner, and I have found an increase of crop by allowing 18 to 21 inches as from plant to plant in the drills. Some will say this is a most expensive seeding, and I agree with them so far. But this seeding only means a few more hundredweights of seed per acre, and it has always meant to me more tons of produce to the acre, and a much healthier crop and better sample, with few chitts or coarse ones: in fact, an ideal crop of potatoes.

Before finishing up with this question of seeding, I would strongly impress upon growers the immense benefit to be derived by repeated changes of seed, which, wherever possible, should be from a severer to a milder climate, say, from high lying lands to lower straths, or, bettter still, from some northern part to the south, as from Scotland to England and Ireland. Some extensive growers of my acquaintance have a quantity of fresh seed from me every year, and to this extent, that they never have unchanged seed for more than three years; and these gentlemen tell me that they have found that it more than pays the extra outlay. And I would further impress upon growers the great importance of buying seed only from those who have made *seed potato growing a speciality*, and by all means to avoid dealers' lots unless it can be shown beyond the shadow of a doubt that they are the thing you want, and have come from someone having a reputation; and to bear in mind that, whenever anyone or anything has made a name, there will be found people ready to offer anything that bears the least resemblance to the thing in question, and ready to tell a specious fable to prove its correct origin.

I would also specially draw the attention of growers to a very pernicious system that has become a very common practice with many. I refer to parties getting hold of a new variety, possibly a small quantity only. and putting these—that is, the tubers bought—into a greenhouse or other artificially heated place, and forcing them to stem prematurely, then breaking off the stems when about 1½ inch in length, planting the stems into small pots, and fostering them in heat until they can be planted out. This process of forcing and sprouting is continued until from four to six crops of sprouts are dealt with; and then the almost exhausted tubers are cut to the last eye and planted. I say such treatment can only have one end—complete ruination to the potato in every way. This system is contrary to all the teachings of nature and common-sense; and I cannot understand how men who ought to know better can see their way to practise it, or to say they do not believe it does harm to the plant as a plant for purposes of propagation. I may be harsh in my judgment, but I can only find two excuses for the individual that does this or advises it—either a lack of knowledge or a desire for gain, without regard to the plant or his neighbour; and I cannot let this pass without a solemn protest, as I feel very much like this—that I am being badly used by those who deal with my potatoes in this way. From the beginning I try, so to speak, to bring my introductions forward in the hardiest way, and for the six or more years they are in my hands before being sent out to the world are grown from whole potatoes, or nearly so, and only those tubers planted that stand on 1⅜-inch riddle, with all those eliminated that do not in every way commend themselves to my judgment. Those, and all that pass the 1⅜-inch, are given to my cattle or pigs. Yes, I often think it is very hard on me and my potatoes, when I read of this and that quantity having been grown from *stems* or *cuttings* of one or other of my potatoes; or someone offering chats under an inch riddle for seed purposes. I say again, I think I am in this way badly used.

CULTIVATION.

Having now settled, at least to our own satisfaction, the class of seed to be planted and the precautions to be observed when buying, the next thing to consider is how and when to plant. If you plant upon the flat, as is common in some parts of England and in gardens all over the country, five to six inches will be found to be a proper depth. I have already given in the parts of this paper dealing with seedings the distance to be observed between the drills and between the plants; and when planting in ridges, as is common in Scotland, I find fairly deep planting beneficial in many ways. In the first place, it is a means of putting the sets beyond the easy reach of the crows; in the second place, it admits of severer harrowing and further cleaning of the land if that is necessary; and in the third place, admits of all the after-work to be done with the least possible disturbance to the plant. In the matter of when to plant, begin with the latest sorts first, and as early as possible after the soil is in proper tilth, and you know by experience that there is no likelihood of the frost being so intense as to reach the sets. I think it is generally known that late potatoes and the most of our second earlies are slow to start growing; so, when planted early, you get the first stem and the benefit of all the vigour that is in the set, and bear always in mind that the condition of the plant, in all the earlier stages of its growth at least, is very much determined by the condition of the set. And, another thing, this early planting allows you to defer harrowing until a great many of the seeds of annual weeds have germinated, and so get destroyed. Or, better still, where growing in ridges is practised, you can circular harrow, and will by remoulding the drills and harrowing again as your judgment directs, do much in the way of cleaning the crop of all kinds of weeds. Very early sorts should be started in boxes, and the planting held over until frost risks are reduced to a minimum; and to ensure regularity of crop great care should be taken to avoid injuring the stems when planting.

With increased experience since I penned this advice regarding early potatoes, I have come to be of opinion, the outcome of longer experience, that all seed potatoes should be boxed, whether lates, midseason, or earlies, as early as possible, but not later than the middle of January. The outcome of my experience with boxed, as against seed stored in the usual way in pits or heaps, is that you have an earlier and larger crop. I also consider, when blight is about, you have an advantage there as well; and a further advantage with boxed seed is that you can always, without losing growth, wait until the land is in that condition of tilth and warmth which every grower knows means so much for health, growth, and consequent yield of his potato crop.

I am decidedly of opinion that hand-hoeing of potatoes, as usually practised, is far from being so beneficial to the potato plant as most cultivators imagine. In fact, I am altogether of opinion that the operation as usually practised is more hurtful than beneficial to the potato plant. Go over a field of potatoes after they have been hand-hoed, and what do you find? Almost every plant showing several inches of white stems, and bared of earth down or almost to the set, stems swayed and swaying about in all directions, leaves hanging limp and withered, the roots in most cases lying bare of earth, and closer examination reveals that the feeders of the plant, the rootlets, are cut and broken, and in many instances, if the crop is slightly advanced, the tuber-bearing stems partially destroyed—all of which means a check of fourteen days or more at the most important period of its growth. In fact, I am altogether of opinion that though the plant seems to get along again, it never really gets over this ill-usage; it is, in short, maimed in a lesser or greater degree for all the days of its life.

In the matter of after-cultivation the whole aim is to keep down the weeds and to foster the plants; and, as I have already informed you, I am opposed to hand-hoeing, at least, as commonly practised. This keeping of weeds in check and of fostering the plants can best be accomplished by going over them with some light implement, such as the Hunter hoe, drawn by one horse, followed by a light moulding plough a few days after. The stirring with the hoe kills all the weeds within an inch or two of the plants, and the slight moulding up with the plough smothers all those untouched by the hoe. These operations of horse hoeing and moulding up can be repeated if necessary. Then let us suppose that everything has been done and the crop is ready for final earthing up, have them as deeply stirred as possible between the drills; then with a Hunter or Newlands moulding plough have them well earthed up. I have no interest in these ploughs, but recommend them as doing their work to my satisfaction; and this last operation is, in my opinion, of the utmost importance, and the well-being of the crop depends more upon this operation being well done than most people imagine. When deeply earthed up, I find the tubers are generally larger and more uniform in size; and there will be less disease among sorts liable to blight if the moulding up is carefully and deeply done, and there are few or none of the tubers green-ended. There is a further and most important advantage, especially to growers of late varieties, the protection it affords to the tubers from early frosts, common enough in Scotland before the late varieties are all harvested.

HARVESTING AND STORING.

The harvesting of earlies is often upon us before the corn crop is in the yard—in some seasons and in some districts long before the reaper is in the fields; in fact, always should be, in the case of early varieties, if the crop is grown for purposes of propagation—that is, for seed. Although not generally known, potatoes of this class—that is, early varieties—should never be allowed to get to full maturity before being harvested if intended for seed purposes—in fact, this applies to all potatoes, whether late, midseason, or early—consequently potatoes grown and dealt with for purely market purposes are quite unfit for seed purposes, although, unfortunately for the commercial grower, the great bulk of the potatoes offered and sold by dealers, seed merchants, and that now very large class calling themselves seed potato growers, are of this class of seed. These latter may be potato growers, but I hold it is the most ridiculous presumption on their part to call themselves *seed potato growers*. That they are anxious to do business and make money thereby is all right for them. I do not mean that there is any dishonesty on their part; but I hold there is the most lamentable ignorance, with little desire to know what is the first essential of the business they seek to follow. They may make money, but the man who grows from this class of seed suffers. So does the potato, that has in its raising cost someone a deal of time, patience, and some little ingenuity. In a word, the potato grown for and dealt with as a commercial product, although it may do fairly well, is yet not well suited, for the reasons given above, for seed purposes. The foregoing remarks, as will be understood, apply wholly to potatoes grown for purposes of propagation, and I may here say that the proper way of storing potatoes intended for seed is by putting them into boxes, and storing away in a well lighted and ventilated house, which can be made frost-proof when the weather is of exceptional severity.

If your house is large, as it must always be where great quantities are stored, I consider it is wise to have a few thermometers hanging about, so that when frost is severe you can see at a glance when you require to use protective means, such as covering up with sacks or canvas, or the lighting up of a few paraffin stoves, but only raising the temperature to 36 or 40 degrees. There is no limit to the height the boxes may be stored but the height of the building. But, to prevent mixing of varieties, put each in a block by itself, leaving a passage between the different kinds. This guards against mixing or confusion, and enables one to see if they are keeping in good order, and also to observe how the different varieties are progressing when they begin to sprout. It often happens that a crop is lifted in what is believed to be a perfectly sound condition, and shortly afterwards it is found that many of the tubers begin to show blight. This, I aver, is caused by the potatoes being brought into contact with disease spores when they are being dug. The best preventative is to have some fresh ground lime, and while the potatoes are still damp and all the earth that is adhering to them as well, is to dust them carefully with lime; or, better still, to have a close-bottomed utensil—say an old riddle with a light zinc bottom—and the potatoes rolled about in this amongst some of the ground lime. Then put them on to a small meshed riddle, give them a shake over, and this will leave the potatoes a slight grey colour. Then put them away in boxes into the store for the winter. With this treatment I think you will find your potatoes keep in a way they never did before: that is my experience. I have been trying this for a number of years, and am so satisfied with results as to recommend it to your consideration and to ask you to give it a fair trial.

In the matter of implements for harvesting or digging the crop, for small growers, or for digging small plots, the 4-pronged fork in the hands of a careful man is difficult to beat; but, to the grower of 20 acres and upwards, this method is out of the question. Many kinds of mechanical diggers have been tried, but the first form—the one with the flat share and back spinner—is still the most popular. There are many makers of this implement, all of which claim some special advantage for their own make. As a user, I like the digger made by Messrs Jack & Sons of Maybole; but at the same time, many very large growers speak highly of those sent out by other firms.

In the storing of commercial potatoes in pits, as we in Scotland call the field stores, but in some parts of England are spoken of as pies or graves, I think growers will find it profitable to have *ground lime* here as well. As the potatoes are brought in, sprinkle the lime freely amongst them, and in particular, previous to covering the potatoes with straw, sprinkle again freely with lime. This will very much prevent the appearance of and spread of blight, as well as a form of skin disease *(tubercinia scabies)* which often appears in potatoes in pits, especially in wet seasons, and under any conditions of weather in potatoes grown on heavy or wet land. I may here remark that I have found the application of ground lime at the rate of 10 cwts. to the acre just before preparing the land for planting have a wonderful effect in preventing the appearance of *tubercinia* in the crops while yet growing—that is, on land liable to show it on the potatoes before harvesting.

The next care is to use plenty of dry hand-thrashed wheat straw, which should be as straight and dry as possible for this purpose, laid thickly and evenly on the angle sides. Put on in this way it sheds off the rain better and keeps the potatoes dry. After having thus covered the sides of the pit or clamp, and just before putting on a little earth to keep the straw in its place, no matter whether the straw you have laid on the sides of the potatoes reaches to the top or even beyond, take an equal thickness of this straight straw and bend it over the top, fixing down on either side with some earth. Potatoes so covered with straw, and six to eight inches of earth, or even less earth, are in a fairly safe condition. From this manner of covering with straw there is little fear of wet getting in; and from the quantity of straw there is enough ventilation to prevent heating. The light covering of earth required with the heavier covering of straw, the straw remains comparatively open; and, further, there is in the majority of our winters little need for covering the top with earth. I seldom have anything else than half dry farmyard litter spread over the ridge. When frost comes for a length of time, or if very severe, I put a little more of this litter on the ridge, and possibly a little on that side of the pit getting most of the north winds. Very rarely have I frosted potatoes, and I might almost say never any frosted in the pits.

THE DEVELOPMENT OF NEW BREEDS OF POTATOES.

PAPER BY MR ARCH. FINDLAY.

From *The North British Agriculturist* of 25th January, 1905.

The fifth of the Glasgow Discussion Society lectures for another season was delivered on Wednesday evening by Mr Arch. Findlay, Mairsland, Auchtermuchty, the subject being as above. Owing to the Vehicles Lighting meeting in Edinburgh on the same afternoon there was a much smaller attendance than usual, and some difficulty at the outset was experienced in getting a chairman. In the end, Mr William Reid, Burnside, Braco, who has himself been growing seed potatoes to some extent, consented to preside. In introducing the lecturer, Mr Reid said that the potato was a plant which had been very much brought before them of recent years, and Mr Findlay was a gentleman who was the very king of the profession. He had introduced more new breeds of the very best kinds than any other man, and he was sure that they would all hear a very interesting lecture.

Mr Findlay, who was very cordially received, said—The subject of my discourse this afternoon is "The Development of New Breeds of Potatoes." As the Chairman has told you, in his all too flattering remarks with regard to myself, my humble endeavours have been to help my fellow-men by giving a little more attention to the potato plant, and on the lines of breeding perhaps somewhat of a kind that had not been much practised until I commenced on lines which I was pleased to flatter myself were systematic—I might almost say scientific, as I understand the word, so far as it applies to the breeding of animals and plants. In a word, my business has been the breeding of potatoes as by nature arranged, though by artificial means, which are neither fantastic nor outrageous to common sense. But more of this later on. In the meantime I will try to tell you how new potatoes were produced in the good old days of, say, fifty years ago. It goes without saying that the world at that time, like ourselves, was younger by that tale of years; but still at that time we thought, and those who were older than I thought, that they did know a thing or two, even about potatoes. But I daresay there would have been considerable opening of eyes and mouths in these days if anyone had talked to the farmer, gardener, or cottager of breeding potatoes, or any other plants, by judicious selection of parent plants, the one to stand in relation to the other as sire and dam. In those days, and I remember of them well, there were just about as many potato apples or plums in a field of potatoes as there were of potatoes. It may be a novel idea, but I am inclined to think that

THE POTATO IN ITS WILD STATE

in South America must have had at some time many enemies, or some circumstance in connection with the climate of its native land that at some time had threatened it with extermination, and set it about to meet the exigency by turning its attention to the production of tubers as a means of carrying on its existence. But, be that as it may, at the time to which I refer all the varieties of potatoes in cultivation grew big crops of plums or apples, and those of you who are old enough will remember how we, as boys, filled our pockets with them, and then found a suitable switch from the nearest hedge, and made a game of trying to throw them farthest from the point of the switch. But then, as now, there was always someone with his top piece so badly got up as to be discontented with things as he found them, or, as possibly some of his neighbours put it, so far left to himself as to pick up some specially large plum, slip it into his pocket, put it away in some old jug in some sand or fine earth. By spring the plum would have rotted away, leaving the potato seeds amongst sand or earth, amongst which he faithfully mixed his onion seed before sowing, thus, in a way, beginning a connection between these two useful plants that did not quite finish here. At least, it was the hope of this early developer that they would in time grace his humble board in still closer connection, only that crop of onions would not be with that potato crop. Now in your mind's eye follow that man when the onions, baby potato plants, and weeds began to show. How carefully he saw to the weeding of that onion bed. Wife nor child was allowed to assist, and the wandering hen or cat soon found out what that man was like in his wrath. How carefully these potato plants were cared for, and I speak from what I have seen. Ever so many of the onions were used as syboes that, but for the potatoes, would have been allowed to live the natural term of their lives. But

THE FASCINATION OF THE POTATO

was on the man, and no care, sacrifice, or labour was too much. And as the mellowing hand of autumn spread its tints of gold and brown, plant by plant was taken up, gloated over with a love, and stored away for another year with a care and fulness of hope that never fell to miser's hoard. For in these few small potatoes were to this man—and there were many such men—all the possibilities, as they understood these things, of that satisfaction too often the only reward of having done some good, not only for themselves, but for their fellow-men. Gentlemen, I say all honour to those men. Most, if not all of them, were of humble life. They did their best according to their lights, and it will be some time yet before the name of Paterson or Nicol is forgotten in this connection. I knew the latter personally, but did not have the good fortune to know Paterson. But I will say this—his potato, the Victoria, was about

THE BIGGEST GIFT EVER BESTOWED

on the human race. I do not now refer to it as a potato—a mere commercial article. I refer to its influence on the potatoes of to-day. Individually, for breeding purposes, I would not give a farthing for any potato if I could not trace its descent from the Victoria, either on the male or female side. And I say again, no man will, by the distribution of mere wealth, though it were a thousand times that of a Rothschild or a Carnegie, do what Paterson has done for mankind. I hold that distribution of mere wealth has a detrimental and pauperising effect, whereas Paterson's potato has led to honest labour, and by labour, prosperity and comfort and the production of untold millions year by year. But again, on the other hand, I have known many men who wrought all their lives on the same lines as Paterson and Nicol, and I daresay brought as much intelligence to bear upon their work as either of these men did, yet never in their lives were they fortunate enough to produce anything of outstanding merit—mediocrity often enough, but that was all. You can well understand there were many thousands doing this same thing all over the country—I mean Scotland, England, and Ireland, leaving out of consideration our continental neighbours and our cousins in America. Then what was the net result? Just enough of merit to keep the plant alive, but with none of that reliance and comfortable assurance the commercial grower likes to have. I am afraid I am encroaching upon your time and patience with this rather mixed up story of the work done by some of my predecessors, but before I get on to

THE CHIEF PART OF MY BUSINESS

here to-night—the story of my own doings with the potato—I will first introduce to your notice some rather novel methods I have seen adopted by some men, of whose intelligence, knowledge, and ingenuity I had a higher estimate before I was let in to this little secret of their doings, with a view to get a fusion of two varieties, in the hope of getting one possessing the best points of both. (Here Mr Findlay showed and explained two halves of different potatoes which had been tied together and planted. In another case the eye of one potato had been taken out and inserted in a potato in which all the eyes were destroyed; he also found two bunches of blossom of two different potatoes tied together that the one might fertilise the other, but did not.) Continuing, he said—There is still another method of getting new varieties which I cannot well pass over, and which we must put to the credit of the intelligence and general smartness of the latter end of the nineteenth and the beginning of the twentieth centuries. A set of men with greedy eyes to the main chance—to use a rather slangy phrase—have got to know that in hybrid potatoes especially there is at all times a tendency to slight variation in appearance, outside of a strong tendency on the part of some varieties to throw sports that have little or no resemblance to the stock in which they appear. I find this latter tendency mostly in hybrids whose parents are furthest apart in character—that is, in habit of growth, colour of blossom and of tuber, shape of tuber, and, say, the one late and the other early. As I have already said, this has called into existence quite a host of up-to-date star-gazers. Now, at this point I will take the liberty of trespassing on your time and patience again so far as to tell you

MY STORY OF THE UP-TO-DATE POTATO

as I know it. It is now eighteen years since I raised it, and twelve years since I sent it out to find its place in the potato world. Now, to begin with, no man, woman, or child beyond myself ever knew how it was bred. And there is another strong point—one of its parents was never sent out by me or given by me to anyone. There is yet another strong point. I have known, and known fairly intimately, the potato world for the last fifty-five years, and I had never seen a potato up to the time I raised the Up-to-Date that at all resembled it in blossom, foliage, or even in general habit of growth, leaving out of the question its great cropping powers. And I have taken special care to make inquiry all over the United

Kingdom, from men who had been life-long enthusiasts in potato culture—many of these men twenty years my senior—if they, up to the time of the introduction of the Up-to-Date, had ever seen a potato that in any way bore a resemblance to it. But I have got one answer from all of them—an emphatic No! Now, how does it happen that there are now so many potatoes that no one seeing them growing side by side—I mean Up-to-Dates and these other so-called newer varieties—can distinguish as to which is which; and when it comes to a trial of powers of production, you will find from the newspaper reports that Up-to-Date shows a crop of, say, 20 tons to the acre; the next one will be one of these indistinguishables with, say, 19¾ tons, and another of the same order with 20¼ tons, and so on over this unique family of potatoes, that even in productiveness do not in reality show any marked difference. But think I hear some one say—But

WHAT ABOUT THE COOKING?

Well, we are accustomed to see occasionally in the newspapers accounts of cooking tests, in which eminent gastronomic connoisseurs give so many points to flavour, texture, dryness, &c., to this, that, and the other of these indistinguishables. Well, gentlemen, there may be some twist in my mental arrangements, and what I am about to say may be the outcome of this bad condition; but, all the same, I often wonder—yes, I must confess to entertaining a desire to know—how many of these points were made by collusion, and sometimes how much by interest or a desire to bring about a something wished for. There is yet something about the Up-to-Date and its counterparts—especially of the Up-to-Date—I have got to tell you. For the question may have presented itself to some of you, or to someone at some time—May not some of those potatoes that are so like Up-to-Date be natural or hybrid seedlings from Up-to-Date? To the first part of this question I say No; its organs of reproduction are 90 per cent. of them malformed. The stamens or pollen cases are small, and never, so far as I have seen, contain one grain of pollen. The pistil is also of the same character. So I say it is an utter impossibility for anyone to have got a natural seedling from it. And these very defects almost

BAR THE WAY TO CROSS-FERTILISATION.

I hardly think it is vanity on my part to say I have had a fairly long try now at this work, and, with all my experience, with all the dexterity that comes of continued exercise of one's ingenuity, the Up-to-Date potato beat me off so far as being able to effect my purpose, compelling me to fall back, as a last resource, on its male parent, or rather a natural seedling from the same. I then effected my object, and got two or three plums. But, as showing how much the Up-to-Date was off this job of seed production, the plums were small, containing few seeds, and of these few only about 53 per cent. germinated. From this confession you will gather that, compared with the introducers of these counterparts of Up-to-Dates—and they are a goodly number now—I am, as an expert in the cross-fertilisation of the potato, very much on the back form. While I am in the

MIDDLE OF MY CONFESSIONS,

I may tell you that often when I feel fagged out and need a refresher, instead of applying to the "Auld Kirk," as many of my fellow-countrymen do, I turn to that portion of the advertisement columns of some paper in which potatoes are much in evidence, or to some enterprising seedsman's catalogue, and in the to me wonderful romances told there of cross-fertilisations effected and brought to fruition, which I in my ignorance had placed amongst the impossibilities—but, all the same, they serve a good purpose—if I do not laugh outright, I have at least a chuckle deep enough to make me feel another man.

As an illustration of the position in which the general cultivator finds himself at the present time, I will now relate a conversation I overheard at the last Smithfield Show in London. I was looking at some implements of which I thought I was likely to be in want, when two farmers, strangers to me, but who seemed to be well acquainted with each other, and both seemed to be potato growers:—"Good morning," calling each other by their Christian names. "Fine show, isn't it?" said the younger of the two. "Great in potatoes, anyhow," replied the elder, looking round at some rather striking displays. "What are you mostly going in for now?" queried the younger. "Well," replied the older one, "I've been atryin' some of the 'Dukes' and some of the 'Earls.'" "And how do you like 'em?" again queried the younger man. "Oh, just middlin,'" replied the older man. "Them be grand new sorts, anyhow, mister. What's wrong with 'em?" was the next query of the younger man. "Well, it be something like this, Tumis," replied the older man. "I got a change of seeds last spring, and I got persuaded to have some of them grand new sorts; and what did I do but planted 'em right in the middle of a field of Dates, thinking as they would be quite safe there. And safe they be, for me or anyone else, for that matter, for I have never been able, since they were taken out of the bags, to say which was which. Rather hard upon an old chap, wasn't it, Tumis?" I did not listen further to their conversation, but went away. Smiling at that time didn't quite give me relief enough. I think I have now said as much as you care to listen to as to these

STRIKINGLY NOVEL METHODS OF DEVELOPING

new varieties of potatoes that have come to be so much in evidence within the last ten years, and shall now proceed to tell you something that I flatter myself I know about the potato plant, in relation to the production and development of new varieties of potatoes. In the first place, I am distinctly of opinion that natural cross-fertilisation never took place in any part of the world at any period of the world's history. The blossom of the potato has a faintly sweet smell, yet it secretes no honey or nectar, and the pollen seems to be a bit too sharp and tasty to suit the palate of even the most voracious insect. In fact, it is highly poisonous, and I daresay that is where their objection comes in. I have seen now and again a humble bee, no doubt attracted by the sweet smell of the blossom, alight on the edge of the petal, but never saw one explore the bloom, as is their habit where they expect to find either nectar or pollen. As the most casual observer will have noticed, the potato is an early closer, shutting up its blossoms between two and three o'clock in the afternoon, and, by reason of a certain twisting process, puts it out of the power of any nocturnal moth or other insect to gain access to either nectar or pollen, even though they both were there. In the second place, I hold it is utterly impossible for the pollen of one blossom to be wind-borne, and so fertilise another, even on the same plant, one reason being that it is too heavy, and another and more important one being that it is a bisexual plant. Both the sexual organs are in the same bloom, the anthers or pollen cases being the male parts, and the pistil representing the female.

And it further appears to me that, for some reason which I have not been able to discover, the potato plant is

BY NATURE OPPOSED TO CROSS-FERTILISATION,

for, immediately the pollen in the anthers is matured, the bloom twists itself up harder than ever round the pistil, and no longer opens out to greet the sun. The bloom then no longer stands erect on its stem, but begins to hang down, swaying in the breeze. The pollen falls down into the narrow space formed by the twisting of the petals all around the bulbous point of the pistil. The bloom thus remains for the matter of two days, and then falls off. Strange to say, the pistil only absorbs a very limited portion of the pollen. Yet what is left, so far as I have been able to discover, is perfectly inert. The potato, as I have already said, is, in my opinion, opposed to cross-fertilisation. It is a well-known fact that the old Blue Don and Paterson's Victoria were both of them free plum bearers. Now, I have castrated blooms on both—that is, removed the pollen cases before they had reached maturity—and then cross-fertilised the Victoria with the Don, and the Don with the Victoria. Of these crossed plums I had 168 seedlings. They all bloomed freely, but only one of these 168 produced plums, and that very sparingly; whereas naturally-produced plums from them both produced fully 50 per cent. of plum-bearing plants. So you will see, although we can improve the potato plant in the direction of hardiness and productiveness, it is at the expense of what is to the plant its

MOST ESSENTIAL FUNCTION—

that is, its natural continuation from true seed. I think, after what I have already said, I need not detain you with an explanation as to the way in which cross-fertilisation is accomplished, nor enter upon the greater question of the varieties that lend themselves best to the process, nor to what varieties you, who are so minded, had better give your attention. For myself, I keep my breeding stock as carefully as any breeder of Aberdeen-Angus cattle or Clydesdale horses. I sell their progeny, but never sell from this stock—I mean, I have never sold any tubers produced by what I term my sires and dams. I do not think there is any special gift required to enable anyone to master the art of cross-fertilisation. But I do think the art of selection of what are to give the best results in the field, the garden, and on the dinner table, will ever be the occupation of a very few. I do not refer to the selection of the potatoes after you have grown them from the seed; I mean the working up of a reliable breeding stock. I hold it is in this direction one's ingenuity is taxed; and, further, one is even the better to know something of the ancestry of a potato. Pedigree, even in a potato, is not to be lost sight of. In short, I feel it is not quite a suitable job for a man or a woman who just knows enough of the vegetable world to distinguish a potato from a turnip. In a word, the mere knowledge not only of potatoes, but of many other things appertaining to natural science, the greater the likelihood of that party's success. It may be of interest to those of you who have got some potato seed if I were to tell you

HOW I DEAL WITH MY OWN.

First, I get a shallow seed pan, such as gardeners use, attend to the drainage, fill it up, or nearly so, with well-decomposed leaf mould, to which has been added a little fine sand. I take a flat piece of wood, and beat it down fairly firm and level, and sow the seeds thinly and evenly over the flat and firm surface. That done, I take and sift, after adding more sand, some more of this leaf mould. The sifting will remove all grit and stones. Now sprinkle a small portion over the seeds, but see that you do it evenly and not over-thick—as near to an eighth of an inch as you can; give also a slight beat down. If the mould is fairly moist, you need not give any water for at least two days. Set your tray, to be out of the way of mishap, into the sunny corner of a cold frame. Put a piece of old newspaper or other paper over the tray, covering up with a piece of glass. Your great care now is to see that you do not allow the earth or mould to get dry; at the same time you must guard against making it too wet. In a week or ten days your seed should begin to braird. You must then give them more light and air. With average care, in a very short time you will have nice plants. When about an inch high, put them out in small pots singly. In another three weeks or so, if the weather is suitable, and the season far enough advanced, plant them out in the open where you mean them to be permanently. After this, your work is all in the ordinary course; only remember this, you must take care when you harvest them to keep the produce of every plant by itself—I mean those you intend to grow again. Fifty per cent. or more will be of no use to go further with; and the 50 per cent. left year by year you, if wise, will further reduce, until at the end of four years you have only one or two left as the sole representatives of your labour and care.

The Chairman, in inviting discussion, said they had all listened to a very interesting paper—a paper which he thought no other man except Mr Findlay could have given them. He thought the lecturer had given away a few of the secrets of the trade.

Mr James Ramsay, Robslea, said the land that he cultivated was not suited for potatoes, and some years he did not harvest as many as he planted. (Laughter.) He had to thank Mr Findlay for his paper. It was the product of thought and of an experience in a field in which there were few of his (Mr Findlay's) equals. Mr Findlay's fame was already great, but he thought if he could produce a potato of the quality of the old Regent, his fame would be assured for many centuries. There was one rather strange thing about potato growing, and that was that thirty to thirty-five years ago they got as good potatoes up to the middle of July, grown within ten miles of Glasgow, as they could get to-day at the same date from Ayrshire. After the first fortnight in Ayrshire it became a glut, and many of the early Ayrshire potatoes were little better than blebs of water. The Red Bog and the old Dalmahoy were good potatoes thirty years ago. Mr Findlay would know that the potato belonged to a family which was largely poisonous, and that was one reason why they got the best quality potatoes after cooking. (Mr Findlay—"Yes, that is so.") (Applause.)

Mr Blair said he was very much indebted to Mr Findlay, but at the same time he had to confess that he was rather disappointed. He expected the lecture to be as it was entitled in the syllabus, and that they were to be shown how to produce a Northern Star or an Eldorado. (Laughter and applause.) He expected to receive a few tips. (Renewed laughter.) He wanted to know if it was the case that, say, they had a plant or a bloom of Up-to-Date, and a bloom or plant of another variety, would they not cross with one another?

Mr Findlay, in reply, said that he had told them he had to go back to a seedling of one of the parents of Up-to-Date before he could get a cross. He was rather surprised at the remarks made by Mr Blair. He thought he had just about laid the whole show bare in his lecture. (Laughter.) He had told them how the modern introducers produced their new breeds. How they went and looked about, and whenever they saw a plant showing the least variation from the main stock, they collared it and sent it out as a new variety. That was a tip for them. (Loud laughter.) He had told them that they had got to get the pollen from the one plant and put it upon the pistil of the other plant when it was ready to receive it; and he had told them when the plant was ready to receive fertilisation. (Applause.) He had no potatoes with him. If he had had any plants with him, he would possibly have given away the business in its entirety. As he was situated then, however, it was a mere case of story-telling. He had, perhaps, failed to impress upon them that this matter of raising new varieties of potatoes possessing extra good productive powers was brought about by the judicious selection of the parents, and not by promiscuously crossing one plant with another. The latter method was no earthly use. They must know what they were doing.

Mr White, Auchens, wanted to know the sire and the dam of Up-to-Date, which was a good potato. What was its number in the stud-books. (Laughter.) Many of the names of the supposed new varieties were new, but the potatoes which bore the names were old enough.

Mr Findlay said he thought Mr White's query was pertinent enough, but he would tell them straight that such matters were trade secrets. (Applause.) He was not prepared to give the whole show away. (Laughter.) His business was to breed potatoes. He had no objection to them doing the same, but he had an objection to telling them straight away and showing them to the very bottom of what had taken him a lifetime to learn himself. (Applause.)

On the motion of the Chairman, a hearty vote of thanks was awarded the lecturer, and the proceedings closed with a vote of thanks to the Chairman, proposed by Mr Blair.

The following editorial appeared in *The North British Agriculturist* of 25th January, 1905 :—

Mr Findlay's lecture at Glasgow on Wednesday last was rather disappointing in some respects. For one thing, the attendance was rather disappointing, as most of the farmers who usually attend the Discussion Society's meeting were on that occasion at the great demonstration in Edinburgh against the Motor Union's Bill. Then the lecture was rather a disappointment to the meeting, as those present had been sanguine enough to expect that the lecturer was to tell them all the secrets of his profession, and show them how they could all raise new varieties of potatoes which they could all sell to each other at fabulous prices. But, with the smile that was childlike and bland, the lecturer told them that he was not to give away any of his trade secrets as to the raising of new varieties, though he would tell them that a vast proportion of the so-called new varieties that were now on the market at high prices were simply old friends with new names. He paid a cordial tribute of respect to the memory of the late Mr Paterson—the father of the potato-raising fraternity. He also expressed in emphatic language his strong conviction that, to vary the words of Dean Swift, the man who raised a new variety which would make two potatoes grow where only one grew before did more good to the community than the multi-millionaire who pauperised people and institutions by his lavish gifts. Of course, that was where the raiser of the Up-to-Date and British Queen came in, for no one questions the great benefit that these varieties have brought to the community of consumers. It was rather a curious coincidence, however, that almost at the very time when the raiser of the Northern Star and the Eldorado was telling the tricks of the potato-raising trade as practised by other raisers, the Tenant-Farmers' Protection Association in Yorkshire were roundly denouncing the "boom" in new varieties of high-priced potatoes as being a thing that the public should be solemnly warned against. One of these denunciators had been greatly disappointed with the yield of the half-tuber he had paid £2 10s for, and that was not to be wondered at, as the half-tuber in question had probably been grown from a second or third crop "shoot," which was the surest way of ensuring failure in the yield. No doubt the "boom" was greatly overdone as regards prices; but last year, on account of the high price of sound tubers, and the huge profits realised by those who had big crops of sound tubers, a perfect frenzy seemed to take possession of growers, and the fortunate holders of the much-boomed new varieties, which were lauded as enormous croppers and proof against disease, could hardly be blamed for trying to get as much as could be got for their precious tubers. But in spite of all this, there remains the fact that any variety of potatoes after being grown for a series of years loses its pristine vigour of growth and capacity for resisting disease, so that the bringing out of new varieties which shall be heavy croppers and vigorous disease-resisters is a most important department of usefulness to the community. Those parties who are thoroughly satisfied with the Up-to-Date or British Queen would do well to remember that these varieties were a great improvement on those in general use at the time that the Up-to-Date and British Queen were brought out, and those who were first in the field with these potatoes, which fairly took the market by storm at the time, were able to secure highly profitable prices for their crops. It has further to be remembered that both the Up-to-Date and British Queen have passed their best stage, and but for the exceptionally fine summer and autumn of last year, they would no doubt have been badly affected with disease. As a matter of fact, the "Dates" and "Queens" grown in the south of England, are going bad very rapidly in the pits as it is. At the present time, potato growers all over the country are very anxiously considering the question as to what variety it will be most profitable for them to plant, and they are rather bewildered by the multiplicity of new varieties now on the market. To invest in a small quantity of one or more new varieties at a reasonable price is a bit of a speculation, but it is a perfectly proper kind of speculation; and may lead to important success, while the risk involved is not great. The raiser of the "Date" and "Queen" has in hand just now some new varieties, notably the "Gold Reef" and the "Diamond Reef," which as heavy croppers fairly eclipse anything he has yet produced—we speak from what we have seen of them growing at Mairsland. The price at which these and other new varieties are put on the market is for the public to determine, and no one need buy any new variety at a price which he considers too high. But if a new variety is to take the market, those who are first in the field with it will find it a very profitable speculation.

HOW NEW VARIETIES OF POTATOES ARE PRODUCED.

MR FINDLAY GIVES SOME HITHERTO UNPUBLISHED PARTICULARS.

(From the "Farmer and Stockbreeder Year Book," 1905.)

It is to the art of the interviewer that the future of public opinion belongs. In our experience we frequently find that the men who know profess such little skill with the pen that they gladly excuse themselves of an invitation to put their views on paper. No man has had greater experience in his own particular line than Mr Archibald Findlay, of Mairsland, Auchtermuchty, the potato raiser, who started what is now an extensive business purely from the love of investigating. He has succeeded in introducing varieties which to a large extent have saved the potato to the farmer and revived the interest which attaches to this crop in the best agricultural districts of the country. A cautious Scot, with the proverbial faculty of thinking before he speaks, time was when his early efforts to improve the potato succeeded in impoverishing himself; but these are days of early struggles which he can look back upon complacently. He has weathered the storm, and now rides upon the wave assured of this fact, that the concentrated experience of close on twenty years, allied to keen observation, have left him the uncrowned king of the potato world. Personally, he is a man of distinctly artistic tastes, as the numerous pictures of his own creation at home testify. Doubtless, the keener observation which is usually credited to the artistic mind has been of immeasurable service to him in his business as a hybridiser and raiser of new varieties. His old place at Markinch was known far and near in connection with such varieties as The Bruce and Up-to-Date, but as business expanded Mr Findlay left the ranks of the tenantry and became the laird of Mairsland, near that tongue-twisting town of Auchtermuchty, in Fifeshire. This change was effected in the year 1900, entering into occupation in 1901. He also purchased in Lincolnshire the farm of Langholme, near Haxey, consisting mostly of silt land. The great impetus that has been given to potato growing in England implies that most of Mr Findlay's business as a seed grower had to be conducted from Scotland. Consequently he thought that instead of the mountain going to Mohammet, Mohammet should reverse the proverbial order and go to the mountain. The result will be that the English grower will be enabled to see without undertaking a lengthy journey just what the wizard of the north is doing.

On a recent occasion we had an opportunity of questioning Mr Findlay with reference to his methods, and the resultant interview enables us to present a few hitherto unknown facts concerning his methods of working—cross fertilising, selecting, and fixing.

AS A HYBRIDIST.

"How long," we asked, "have you been hybridising potatoes?"

"Let me see," said Mr Findlay reflectively, "I think I have had about twenty-eight years at the very shortest time as a hybridiser. I started it as an amusement, but I became thoroughly convinced that something had to be done with the potato. All the potatoes that were being sent out seemed to fall short of what I had heard spoken of, in cropping and quality, previous to the blight of 1846."

"What like was the potato when you began?"

"Well of course we had the Magnum Bonum and Victoria and Champion. All these potatoes, so far as I could understand, however satisfactory, were chance seedlings. None of the men who introduced them could be strictly called hybridists, and none of our British insects frequent the potato plant either in search of honey or pollen; consequently, from the very nature of the bloom or blossom and the heavy character of the pollen at the period of fertilisation, it is utterly impossible that the pollen could be carried by the wind. I have never seen any reason to alter my opinion thus early formed."

HIS FIRST SUCCESS.

"What was your first success?"

"The Bruce," was the emphatic rejoinder. "Previous to that I had contented myself with ordinary horticultural varieties for prize-taking, &c. I thought it was emphatically necessary that something should be done for agriculture. The Bruce potato was the result of cross fertilisation of the Late Rose and the old Victoria, then decidedly past its best, but still very generally grown.

"The Victoria was in reality the first potato that was introduced since the period of the blight that stood out against the ravages of the disease in any marked way. I thought that by judicious blending of this special character with something more prolific should (and my knowledge of cross-bred animals and plants led me to reason that the chances were all in favour, by union of the bloods of these two so distinct varieties of the potato) result in something of superior excellence. I may tell you this," continued our informant, "as an omnivorous reader, with decided interest in all things appertaining to plants and animals, I had studied the lessons of Bakewell and also growers of new varieties of cultivated plants. That gave me courage; in fact," and here the enthusiast spoke, "so inspired me with that spirit of perseverance and patience that marked those men that I quite resolved to devote a considerable portion of my time to see what could be done with this special plant."

EARLY DIFFICULTIES.

"Have you any reminiscences about your early triumphs?"

"Well, when we introduced The Bruce we could not get anyone to take it up. I offered it to most of the leading seedsmen of that day and got little or no response. However, I got some farmers I was acquainted with to pay 12s 6d per cwt. and take them up. I thought it was very big money," continued our host, with a smile engendered by recollections of the prices current during the present boom. "And," he continued, "immediately they were grown by these men they not only impressed them but became the talk of the country; and, as fortune would have it, we had a night of severe frost in September that cut down the

Magnums and Champions, while The Bruce came out of the ordeal comparatively scathless by reason of the density of the foliage. Well, that was a feather in the cap of The Bruce. A potato that would grow on and mature itself after such an ordeal as that rather struck them as a thing to be desired, and that enabled me to sell my potatoes of that year's produce twenty or thirty times more at the enhanced price of 18s to 20s per cwt. In fact, that success paved the way for all my future successes."

WHEN UP-TO-DATE APPEARED.

"Then after that?"

"My next epoch-maker was Up-to-Date. We introduced several others which commanded considerable attention, but as an outstanding maincropper Up-to-Date was the next success. As showing, however, the commotion which The Bruce had made, when I began to offer Up-to-Date every grower of these asked me if it was better than it; and when I assured them that it was, they simply went away shaking their heads and smiling in derision. However, the sequel proved that I was right. The Bruce had passed its stage of vigour and usefulness, and then the Up-to-Date, although of different shape, and not of the exact shape that markets had been accustomed to, by reason of its enormous cropping power simply swept the show. Although, I may tell you, that I lost all the coppers I made off The Bruce to introduce the Up-to-Date. In fact," said Mr Findlay frankly, "it was only when it came to be universally known that I was able to recoup myself of the money I had spent in trying to introduce that potato. The signal success of the Up-to-Date when it got into general cultivation set, as one would say, the gate as wide as it could be for any future introduction that I could place before the farmer. Since then British Queen, Evergood, Challenge, Royal Kidney, the Goodfellow, and Northern Star, and several others have followed. And now I am introducing the Eldorado, Millionmaker, and others. I withstood all blandishments to put the Eldorado on the market earlier, because I had never been satisfied that the Eldorado had attained to the purity I wanted. Something was amongst them that did not improve them, although I had rogued them severely. I withstood all blandishments last year until I had grown them again and was able to present them in the condition it was desirable to the farmer."

SYSTEM OF CROSSING.

Questioned with regard to the system he pursued in cross-breeding, Mr Findlay said, "Simply pollinating one plant with another. But the art of pollinating is not the crux of the situation; it is the selection of the varieties and the plants from which to cross-fertilise. I think the great drawback with other men that I know is, either through lack of ability or some other cause, they fail to recognise what are the right plants to use as parents. I hold that the whole of my success has been through the inborn, almost intuitive, faculty of choosing proper parents."

CARE IN SELECTING.

"What method do you pursue when establishing a potato?" we questioned.

"Well, of course," replied Mr Findlay, "we sow the seed first. The progress of the seedlings is a matter we watch with very great care. In their growth and during the autumn disease is always about, and we note how they stand up against attacks of disease. That is the first thing we have to consider in selection. If they go down with disease in the first year, that means they go down for ever. We go for shape and quantity at the roots. Size we do not, however, much consider in the early stage. It is the general shape and balance, uniformity and number, which means that it is prolific as a tuber bearer. All the meaner kinds are discarded that year, or as far as we think is judicious. No special care is taken of them, because the test of every potato is how it will stand the test of field cultivation. We plant them out with ordinary care, and leave them to fight the battle under ordinary conditions in which potatoes have to be grown. Then I personally see to them, studiously watching their growth, periods of blossom, and ripening off; then we go on to the ripening time and we notice how they die off. We never allow them to die down fully. I am now entering into the phase of how potatoes that are grown for seed purposes ought to be dealt with. We dig these potatoes when they have reached what we would call the stage which shows that the fulness of their growth is past, and they are getting into the sear and yellow stage of foliage. But we never allow them to get into the dead stage. I may say that all tubers grown for seed potatoes ought to be harvested at that stage, not when they are full matured. But to return to the seedlings. The ground is all measured on which they are grown, and the crops are duly compared in every way as to shape and amount of produce. The infirm things are all discarded and sent to the pigs. From our long experience of potatoes I think we have then arrived at a very clear conclusion as to their future prospects."

CUT SEED.

Turning to the question of cut seed, we asked whether in propagating new varieties he cut the seed.

"We cut as little seed as ever we possibly can," was the reply. "I also, as I have said, believe that potatoes ought to be lifted, when they are for seed purposes, before they are fully matured. Instead of being stored in pits they should be stored in trays and kept in a place where the temperature is low, but where it can never fall to freezing point. They are looked over several times during the winter and early spring to see how they are keeping and how they are showing evidence of germination. The next thing to be considered by the man that is going to plant is, how little injury by breaking off the stem can be done. That is to say, the first stem that appears before it is planted after sprouting. I hold that every stem that is broken off is a certain percentage of the potato's vitality gone."

"Do you sprout all yours?"

"Mostly, and in boxes. The late varieties do not sprout much; the earlier ones sprout freely."

"How many years does it take you to fix a potato?"

"We always reckon six years at the very earliest."

"Do you find that after a variety has been put upon the market much roguing has to be done?"

"Well, you know that when you get into quantity and employ a great number of people in harvesting, it is then that much mischief is done. They are ignorant of the lines upon which you are doing your business, and even when they wish to do their best for you they pick out potatoes which they should not. They also pick up a potato that does not belong to the crop, and no power on earth will prevent that."

THE FARMER AND NEW VARIETIES.

"What is the farmer's position with reference to new varieties?"

"I think the farmer should investigate much more than he has done; try, in a small way, the new varieties, and then find out those varieties that suit his land and climate best."

"What kind of soil do you raise your new varieties on?"

"I think that is outside of the question. You must have the potato that grows anywhere."

EXPRESS CULTURE.

"Do you believe in the system known as 'express culture'?"

"No. I have already explained that the more you take from a potato means the lessening of its vitality. Then I hold by this that, if we are anxious to improve on nature, nature, given a fair chance, does not make many mistakes. Now, in the tuber is stored up a certain amount of plant food which is necessary to the plant till it reaches that stage when it is able to cater for itself. I am much of the opinion that the man who tries to grow by 'express' culture is much like the man who tries to bring up young animals without milk. I hold that it means ruination for the tuber. I think it is a very regrettable thing to think that I have spent a life trying to make and build up this plant, and immediately they get hold of it they set about undoing the work I have been trying to do."

"Then you think it shortens the life of a tuber to hothouse it?"

"That is so, and makes it so very susceptible to disease and other infirmities."

With that the conversation ended.

APPENDIX.

The Potato "Up=to=Date."

(From *The North British Agriculturist* of 3rd October, 1894.)

The Fifeshire village of Markinch, which formerly had a unique reputation for the monster cabbages and cauliflowers grown in its gardens, and which in recent years has earned a solid and enduring reputation on account of its being the rearing-ground of The Bruce, Her Majesty, and many other new varieties of disease-resisting potatoes, was on Saturday last the scene of an enthusiastic gathering of agriculturists, who had come to take part in Mr Findlay's annual "field day" for inspecting his new varieties of potatoes before these were harvested for the season. The weather was very suitable for the occasion, as it was dry and crisp, and very favourable for completing the ingathering of the cereal crops in the later parts of "The Kingdom." As usual there was a large and representative gathering of agriculturists at this function, which might well be called a full-dress rehearsal of the drama which Mr Findlay is about to produce for the benefit of potato growers all the world over. Unfortunately, one of the members of the Royal Commission on Agriculture, namely, Mr Gilmour, of Montrave, was unable to be present at this gathering in the "land of Moss Rose and The Bruce," as he had a prior engagement which could not be deferred. But, although the unavoidable absence of the laird of Montrave was greatly regretted by the company, the Royal Commission was duly represented by one of the Sub-Commissioners, namely, Mr James Hope, East Barns, Dunbar, who is known over all the country as one of the most extensive and most successful potato growers in Scotland. Mr Findlay's new varieties of disease-resisting potatoes are being very largely grown in the English counties, so much so that many Scottish growers declare that the use of these disease-resisting varieties south of the Border has been a potent source of depression to potato growers in Scotland, through the vast increase of the English output, and the consequent reduction in price. But, all the same, the high favour with which Mr Findlay's new varieties are now regarded was duly vouched for by the fact that at the Markinch gathering on Saturday the Liverpool Farmers' Club was represented by three well-known potato growers, namely, Mr Smith, Moorfields; Mr Cropper, Melling; and Mr Scotston, Gateacre.

Among the local gentlemen present were Mr James Fyshe, J.P., Treaton, who, together with Mr Hope, was a staunch and true friend to Mr Findlay before the value of that gentleman's work had been fully recognised by the country; Mr William Taylor, of Bankhead, Thornton; Mr Cuthbert, of the Dalmeny Estates Office, representing Lord Rosebery; Mr M'Jaunet, the indefatigable advocate of the weigh-bridge, and the sworn foe of the "dials"; Mr Tod, of Pardovan; Mr Alexander Bisset, late of Balfarg, and now of Glenearn; Mr Stewart, of Lindores; Mr Braid, Abercrombie; Mr Marshall, of the Wynton Manure Company, Dundee; Mr J. Hunter, F.I.C., F.C.S., district analyst for Midlothian, and examiner in agricultural chemistry in Edinburgh University; and Mr D. Young, *N.B. Agriculturist*. It was a source of deep and genuine regret to the company to learn that Mr Lawson, the genial laird of Carriston, another enthusiastic supporter of Mr Findlay, was unable to be present this year on account of illness. Among the letters of apology for absence was one from Mr James Stenhouse, of Turnhouse, Cramond, who wrote as follows:—"I am sorry that I will not manage to be present, but I cannot help expressing my opinion that you deserve the thanks of agriculturists in all potato-growing districts for your untiring energy in discovering and selecting new varieties, a labour which has resulted in immense benefit to the farmer, and, I sincerely trust, in pleasure and profit to yourself." Another of the letters of apology was from Mr D. Inglis, agent for Earl Grey, Howick, Northumberland, who said in his note:— "Your Jeanie Deans and Thane of Fife are truly splendid; but the Up-to-Date you sent me for trial I consider perfection. It has great disease-resisting power, a very heavy cropper, and its cooking qualities, I am sure, will suit the most fastidious. As to its keeping qualities I cannot speak, as they were so good I could not manage to keep them from the cook."

On arriving at Markinch, where they were cordially received by Mr Findlay, the first move of the party was to a small field adjoining the station, where Mr Findlay had two of his new varieties growing, namely, Farmer's Glory and British Queen. These are new and very promising varieties which are not on the market yet, though Mr Findlay will be able to spare a few of them this year. Farmer's Glory was found to be a very heavy cropper, and a beautifully shaped potato it is. British Queen was about equally promising as a cropper, and is equally attractive in appearance, and both varieties were found to be absolutely clear of disease.

The party next proceeded to Mr Findlay's garden in Markinch, where a number of his seedlings were growing. Mr Findlay explained that if disease was to be found anywhere in "The Kingdom" it would be in that garden, as the soil was exceedingly rich on account of the yearly accumulation of manure. It was found that many of the seedlings were very promising, and with one or two exceptions they were all quite free from disease; but, of course, they require to be grown for several years before the type is fixed and before the merits of the new varieties can be accurately estimated. One rather novel experiment was also noted with much interest in another garden also held by Mr Findlay. On the one side of the hedge a new variety of potato, called the Exhibitor, was grown, and was manured solely by Patent Silicate Manure; while on the other side of the hedge the same variety was grown manured with farmyard manure. In the patch grown with farmyard manure the tubers were larger and more numerous than on that grown with the silicate manure; but Mr Findlay expressed the opinion that the crop grown with the silicate manure was of better quality than those grown with farmyard manure.

The party next mounted their brakes and drove to Treaton, some three miles distant, where a large breadth of the Up-to-Date variety, which is the trump card in Mr Findlay's hand at present, is being grown for him by Mr Fyshe. Treaton is a high-lying and rather exposed farm, but through the enterprise and good management of Mr Fyshe is kept at the very highest pitch of productive fertility. The party proceeded to the field in front of the farm-house, where the potatoes were growing. This field was a large one of some 34 acres, and the lower half of it, with the exception of a small part at one side, was all under Mr Findlay's Up-to-Date variety, the rest of the field being Maincrops. The field, though somewhat steep, sloped beautifully to the south, and, though not of the best of quality of land naturally, it had evidently been thoroughly well cultivated and manured, and not a weed was to be seen in it. The local visitors were all unanimous in declaring that up till the morning of Thursday last, when the shaws were rather cut down with the frost, this field presented about the finest appearance of any potato field in "The Kingdom." On the lower half, where the Up-to-Dates were grown, the crop had received a full dressing of farmyard manure, but no artificials; but on the upper half, where Mr Fyshe's own Maincrops were grown, the crop had received 3 cwt. per acre of Messrs J. & J. Cunningham's special potato manure in addition to the farmyard manure. The Maincrops and Up-to-Dates were both found to be heavy crops; but the Up-to-Date variety had decidedly the advantage in respect of yield, while they were equally attractive in appearance. Every shaw of this Up-to-Date variety showed an average of from nine to twelve market potatoes. In respect to their quality, Mr Smith, of Moorfields, Liverpool, showed a rather novel test which is adopted in the Liverpool market. The test consists in cutting a tuber right through the middle, and rubbing the two sections together, the quality of the potato being indicated by the thickness of the floury paste which shows at the edges when the two sections are again placed *in situ*. Judged by this test, Mr Smith said he had no hesitation in pronouncing the quality of the Up-to-Date to be excellent. Mr Findlay also showed another test, which he has found to be very reliable. This test consists in cutting a thin section of the tuber and laying it against some dark substance, and the proportion of floury substance in the potato is shown by the clearness and prominence or otherwise of the starch-cells in its composition. In this field there was also a drill each of Farmer's Glory and British Queen, as well as of Goodhope and Lady Rosabelle, two other varieties which are yet in the initiatory stage, and all of which were very promising.

Having completed the inspection of the crop, the party drove back to Markinch, where a sumptuous lunch had been provided for them in the Bethune Arms. Mr Hope, East Barns, occupied the chair, and Mr Fyshe, J.P., acted as croupier. The potatoes served at the dinner consisted of Farmer's Glory, British Queen, and Up-to-Date, and all were found to be of superlatively high quality as table varieties. The Chairman, in giving the toast of "The Queen," said he hoped it would be as much appreciated as the British Queen had been that day by the company. Needless to say that this toast was enthusiastically pledged.

The Chairman then gave the toast of "Health and Success to Mr Findlay." In speaking to this toast, Mr Hope referred to the representative character of the gathering, who had been drawn there by the great interest they all had in the work Mr Findlay had been carrying on, of providing them with new varieties of superior and disease-resisting potatoes. For himself, he had been greatly impressed with the merits of the Up-to-Date variety, which had proved itself to be quite as heavy a cropper as The Bruce, and was even better in quality. He trusted that Mr Findlay would continue to meet with more and more success in carrying on his work, and he could not help saying that he thought the Board of Agriculture should make some suitable recognition of the importance and value of the work Mr Findlay was carrying on for the benefit of farmers. (Applause.)

Mr Findlay, in responding to this toast, which was received with great enthusiasm, said he was very proud of the large and influential company that had that day come to his annual inspection. He had made it the work of his life to propagate and bring out new varieties of potatoes, and he was very proud of the success he had met with, and for that success he was in a large measure due to the influential support received from some of the principal potato growers in the country, and notably from Mr Hope and Mr Fyshe. For himself he felt very confident that some of the varieties they had seen that day, such as Up-to-Date and Farmer's Glory, would give as much satisfaction as The Bruce or any other variety he had ever brought out. He was specially pleased that Messrs Smith, Cropper, and Scotston, representing the Liverpool Farmers' Club, had come all that distance to be with them that day, as potatoes grown in the hard climate of Markinch and Treaton would, he was sure, give great satisfaction in England. (Applause.)

Mr Fyshe said he could endorse what Mr Findlay had said as to the success that The Bruce and other new varieties of potatoes raised at Markinch had achieved in the hands of English growers. For himself, he had that morning received an offer of £6 per ton for a lot of potatoes of the Jeanie Deans variety, and that price was not so bad. (Laughter.) He would ask them to drink a bumper to the health of these English friends, and at the same time invite them to state what their impressions were of the potatoes they had seen that day.

Mr Smith, Moorfields, Liverpool, said he had been greatly impressed with the grand yield and beautiful appearance of Up-to-Date. The great question for the potato grower of Great Britain was how to produce the heaviest crop of the best quality of potatoes, and it seemed to him that the sorts they had seen that day were admirably suited for attaining that end. Scotch potatoes had a great reputation, not only in the markets of England, but in the markets of the world. As an instance of that, he might state that some potatoes were last year shipped to New York from Glasgow, and some from the same lot were railed on to Liverpool, where they too were shipped to New York. The result was that the potatoes shipped from Glasgow realised 25 per cent. more in the New York market than those from Liverpool, as these latter were looked upon as being English potatoes.

Mr John Hunter, in proposing the toast of "The Press," said that the agricultural community was greatly indebted to the agricultural press for placing before them, in an attractive form, every fact which was likely to be of use to them in their business. Mr Findlay was carrying on a series of practical experiments which were of great value to the country, and were much more worthy of recognition and support from the Board of Agriculture than some of those experiments that were being supported with liberal grants from that Board. The Board had also been plagiarising other people's work, such as Miss Ormerod's, and sending it out as the work of their own officials; and it was the duty of the agricultural press to thoroughly expose that form of literary piracy. He coupled with the toast the name of Mr D. Young, *N. B. Agriculturist.*

Mr Young, in responding, said he quite agreed with Mr Hope in holding that the work which Mr Findlay was carrying on for the benefit of agriculturists was worthy of recognition and assistance from the Board of Agriculture. Dean Swift had laid down the axiom that the man who made two ears of corn or two blades of grass to grow where only one grew before was a true benefactor to his country. And in the same way, the man who made two potatoes to grow where only one grew before, or who made even one potato of a better quality to grow where only one grew before, was a true benefactor of his country.

Mr Taylor, Bankhead, said that they had that day been honouring a gentleman who was doing a great deal of good for the farmers of the country. There was another gentleman there that day who had also been working with the greatest enthusiasm, and in a most disinterested way for the farmers, and that was their friend Mr M'Jannet, of weigh-bridge fame. He begged to propose that they dedicate a bumper to the health of Mr M'Jannet. (Applause.)

Mr M'Jannet, in responding, said he could not do anything to show farmers how to make the most of their potato crops. Last year he called upon a farmer and found him busy at his potato pits, as he had got an order for three tons of potatoes at £2 10s per ton. The farmer was filling his potatoes into bags. He had the bag on the steelyard, and just as it had about reached the weight of 1¼ cwt. he took five potatoes and put three of them into the bag which turned the scale, and then he threw the other two back into the heap. Now the farmer could take that trouble in regard to a very lb. of potatoes, when potatoes were only worth £2 10s per ton, and yet he would not bother himself to find out the weight of his cattle, which were worth £40 per ton! And that was simply a sample of what prevailed among farmers generally. Last year he had at his farm seventeen farmers from Fifeshire, and these men paid over £10,000 of rent per annum in the aggregate. He showed them a nice bullock, and asked them to estimate its dead weight. One farmer was 1¼ cwt. short of the weight, and one man was within 2 lbs. of the exact weight; but on the average all the farmers present were 60 lbs. short, and, at 6d per lb. dead weight, that was equal to 30s in money, which was too much to lose on a single beast. If they would be as careful about the selling of their cattle by weight as they were about the selling of their potatoes, he was confident they would make much more of their cattle than they did.

Mr Fyshe, in proposing the health of the Chairman (Mr Hope), said that Mr Hope's farming at East Barns, where he had a farm of 1000 acres, rented at £5000, was a perfect object lesson in high and successful farming. (Applause.)

Mr Hope, in responding, said Mr Fyshe had spoken of his farming in far too flattering terms, for he had great advantages in regard to soil and climate, which should not be overlooked.

Mr Findlay said they could not part without drinking a bumper to the health of his friend and everyone's friend, Mr Fyshe, who had justly enough eulogised Mr Hope's farming, but who seemed to have forgotten that his own was not very far behind. (Applause.)

Mr Fyshe briefly responded, and the party then broke up, all being highly pleased with the day's inspection.

A Day with Findlay at Markinch.

(From *The Scottish Farmer* and *The Farming World* of 5th October, 1894.)

Mr A. Findlay, Markinch, is fairly entitled to the distinguished honour of being the prince of potato rearers in the whole world. He has, it may truly be said, made it the study of his life to place upon the market the best disease-resisting varieties which can be raised in the British Isles. That he has met with success has been amply proved. Not only have the principal British growers come to him year after year for their seed, but he has been patronised by farmers on the Continent and in America. Wherever his potatoes have gone they have done well, and if he had only produced The Bruce, his name deserved to be held in remembrance. The annual exhibition of his potatoes as they grow in the fields took place on Saturday, when there was a large turn-out of gentlemen from many parts of the country. Among those present were:—Mr James Hope, East Barns, Dunbar; Mr John Cropper, Pinch House, Melling, Liverpool; Mr John Smith, Holly Tree, Grange, near Birkenhead; Mr T. W. Cuthbert, representing Lord Rosebery, Dalmeny; Professor John Hunter, chemical examiner, Edinburgh University; Mr M'Jannet of Over-Inzievar; Mr James Fyshe, C.C., of Treaton; Mr Duncan Stewart, Grange, Newburgh; Mr Alexander Bisset (late of Balfarg), Markinch; Mr Tod of Pardovan; Mr Braid, Abercrombie; Mr W. Taylor, Bankhead; Mr J. S. Marshall, manufacturer, Dundee; Mr J. E. Scotson, Holt Hall, Gateacre, near Liverpool.

Arriving at Markinch station, the company were conducted to a small field a little way off, in which were growing various of Mr Findlay's new sorts. The ground was highly suitable for the purpose. It had not been manured for about thirty years, and was not in a high state of cultivation, so that the new varieties were put to the test. Farmer's Glory—a recent addition to Mr Findlay's new potatoes—was dug up in various parts, and in nearly every instance the result was a satisfactory yield of good, marketable tubers. The experts on the ground—English as well as Scotch—were unanimous in their verdict that Farmer's Glory is a potato which is bound to do well in the British market. Then sound shaws of British Queen—a nice round potato of unquestionable quality—were turned up, and there was ample evidence in all we saw to convince us that it is a first-rate cropper. Several drills of the kidney variety were shown the company; but as they have not yet been brought to perfection we need say no more than that they give promise of being on an equality with the other potatoes reared by Mr Findlay. Moving next to ground on the north side of Markinch, the company was shown The Exhibitor growing under different conditions. In the one case Mr Findlay's ordinary mixture of artificial manures was used, while in the other the ground had been treated with silicate. In our opinion the former yielded the best crop—a result which might reasonably be expected on ground that was only of middling quality. The Exhibitor, however, promises to be worthy of the name which has been given it. The gentlemen of the party also had the opportunity of seeing potatoes grown from seed extracted from the potato apple.

A short halt was made for luncheon at Mr Findlay's residence, where it was intimated that letters of apology for absence had been received from a number of leading agriculturists, including Mr J. Gilmour of Montrave; Mr A. Drysdale, manager for Lord Rosebery; Mr T. Clayton, Spalding; Mr James Macdonald, secretary, Highland and Agricultural Society; Mr W. J. Gulland, Musselburgh; Mr A. Hutcheson, Perth; Mr P. Mitchell, Meiklour, Perth; Mr David Inglis, manager for Earl Grey, Howick Gardens, Lesbury, Northumberland; Mr James Stenhouse, Cramond; and others. The party were then driven in brakes to Mr James Fyshe's farm of Treaton. Here the potatoes were grown under ordinary cultivation. One field had lain out in grass for three years, and the other for one year longer. Farmyard manure was applied in both cases at the rate of about fifteen tons per acre, and the land was clear of weeds, and appeared to be thoroughly well farmed. Farmer's Glory, when turned up at various points, appeared to great advantage, and is a potato which is difficult to beat for quality and quantity. Goodhope, a potato so named a year ago in honour of the tenant of East Barns, made a splendid appearance. It is a prolific cropper, and is one of the best cooking varieties grown, while it also enjoys immunity from disease. Up-to-Date is a potato which has been very appropriately named. Mr Findlay's maincrop potatoes are certainly as good as could be desired. All round he has now as fine varieties on hand as any farmer could desire to choose from, and we hope that those we have just mentioned will continue the fame which he acquired in raising The Bruce, Her Majesty, Jeanie Deans, and many others.

Returning to Markinch, the party were entertained to dinner by Mr Findlay in the Bethune Arms Hotel, where specimens of the potatoes referred to were served up cooked. Mr James Hope presided, and Mr James Fyshe acted as croupier.

The Chairman, in proposing Mr Findlay's health, said he was sure they were all pleased to be present that day to see the work that their friend had been engaged in, and it must have been very pleasant for that gentleman to observe that there were representatives from the agricultural interest, the landlords, and the trading community. (Applause.) Not only so, they had gentlemen from different parts of England—(more applause)—who were engaged in the potato trade, and he hoped that the varieties which Mr Findlay had shown would prove to be a great success. (Applause.) He trusted that some of them would take the place of The Bruce yet. He was remarkably pleased with Up-to-Date, and it seemed to him a potato that would beat The Bruce. (Hear, hear, and applause.) The gentlemen present were not only indebted to Mr Findlay, but he thought the country at large were indebted to him. He trusted that gentleman would long be able to carry on his labours, and he would like to see the heads of the Government rewarding him with a professorship or in some other suitable way. (Loud applause.) He proposed success to their host. (Applause.)

Mr Findlay, in the course of his reply, returned thanks for the honour they had conferred on him in being present, and stated that a large measure of friendship had been meted out to him from first to last in his endeavours to promote potato culture. He gratefully acknowledged the teaching and guidance he had received from Mr John Hunter, and the valuable assistance he had from the first got from Mr Fyshe. It would ever be his endeavour to raise the best possible quality of seed potatoes. (Loud applause.)

Other toasts followed.

Almost similar reports were published by *The Mark Lane Express, Bell's Weekly Messenger, The Agricultural Gazette, The Farmer and Stockbreeder, The Cable,* and all the leading agricultural and other newspapers at home and abroad, which we would have been glad to quote had the proportions I had assigned to this book admitted of my doing so.

Potato Growing in Scotland.

(From *The Farmers' Gazette* of 20th October, 1894.)

Many of the valuable sorts of potatoes that have been raised in recent years having originated in Scotland, and such a large proportion of the seed used every year by the farmers of Ireland coming from that country, the following resumé of the annual inspection of a potato grower's farm will prove of interest. Mr Archibald Findlay, of Markinch, Fifeshire, the successful raiser of The Bruce and other famous varieties of potatoes, it will be seen still continues his efforts in the production of new varieties of potatoes, many of them giving excellent promise of successful results. On the 29th ult., Mr Findlay, in accordance with his annual custom, had a large attendance of gentlemen interested in potato culture to inspect his crops of the different varieties of potatoes. In looking over the list of names as published in *The North British Agriculturist, Dundee Courier,* and other local papers, we find a number of representative men from England, but not one from Ireland, which, in connection with a subject of such great importance, was surely an omission which should be rectified in future years. Samples of each variety were lifted in presence of the company, so that by personal inspection at the instant of raising, each member of it could judge for himself as to its cropping capability and disease-resisting power.

Proceeding to the garden, the first variety tested was that of England's Glory, a potato raised by Mr Findlay, but not yet in the hands of the public. Several stalks were dug at different points over the plot; in some of them as many as twelve fine-looking tubers being turned out, of fine shape, and with no appearance of a taint. The next of the new varieties shown was the British Queen; like the other, not yet on the market; but a most promising variety, the tubers being of attractive shape, and of excellent flavour when cooked. A number of other varieties were shown; none of them yet on the market, but most of them promising to be useful. Plots were shown where potatoes were grown with different kinds of manure, bulky and concentrated, the results in nearly every instance being in favour of the former, either entire, or assisted by a portion of artificials; the quality, however, being in favour of those grown with patent silicate manure.

The company in the course of the day went to the farm of Treaton, about three miles distant from Markinch—a high-lying farm, tenanted by Mr James Fyshe, an eminent farmer and potato grower. A field of thirty-four acres on this farm was under potatoes, consisting of only two varieties—Up-to-Date and Maincrop, the Champion, without which no ordinary Irish farmer can get on, being no longer a favourite in Scotland. The field, although not naturally fertile land, had all the appearance of thorough cultivation and liberal manuring, and not a weed was to be seen. Two mornings before the haulms had been cut down by frost; but the local visitors were unanimous in declaring that previously it had the finest appearance of foliage of any field over the entire "Kingdom": this high-sounding title still clinging to historical Fife, as it does to our own picturesque "Kingdom of Kerry." A few stalks here and there of each kind were lifted, the Maincrops and Up-to-Dates being both excellent crops—the latter, however, having an apparent advantage in respect of yield, while equally attractive in appearance. As in Mr Findlay's garden, a portion of the field crop was grown with different manures—farmyard and artificials, and their combinations, the exact results from each being most instructive to growers if published.

After the luncheon, which was of a sumptuous character, the speeches were more or less confined to the subject of potato growing and the most profitable markets for their disposal. Mr M'Jannet was exceedingly happy in his illustration of the care with which a farmer usually weighs a sack of potatoes, worth a few shillings, while he takes chance for the weight and value of a fat beast worth many pounds.—RUSTICUS.

Important Inspection of Potatoes in Fife.

(From the *Dundee Advertiser* of 1st October, and *People's Journal* of 6th October, 1894.)

On Saturday a large company of agriculturists, potato merchants, and others from various districts of Scotland and England, met at Markinch, by invitation of Mr A. Findlay, the successful potato grower, to examine his crop of potatoes on various fields in the district. The company included Mr James Hope, East Barns, Dunbar; Mr John Cropper, Pinch House, Melling, Liverpool; Mr John Smith, Holy Tree, Grange, near Birkenhead; Mr T. W. Cuthbert, representing Lord Rosebery, Dalmeny; Professor John Hunter, chemical examiner, Edinburgh University; Mr M'Jannet of Over-Inzievar; Mr James Fyshe, C.C., of Treaton; Mr Duncan Stewart, Grange, Newburgh; Mr Alexander Bisset (late of Balfarg), Markinch; Mr Tod of Pardovan; Mr Braid, Abercrombie; Mr W. Taylor, Bankhead; Mr J. S. Marshall, manufacturer, Dundee; Mr J. E. Scotson, Holt Hall, Gateacre, near Liverpool; Mr Young, *N. B. Agriculturist;* Mr Mowat, &c. Mr Findlay awaited the arrival of the party at the railway station, Markinch, and conducted them to an extensive field adjacent. A number of shaws of Farmer's Glory were dug up at different parts of the field. The shaws stood about 34 inches, and the potatoes at the roots numbered 10—sometimes more and sometimes less. They were in fine marketable condition, and the experts pronounced favourably on them. Mr Findlay stated that he had only got the field in spring, and that it had not been "dunged" for thirty years. British Queen was also exhibited in the same way. It was stated to be a very fair sample of potato, and a grand cropper. The Exhibitor was dug up in ground to the north of Markinch. Manure had been used at one part and silicates at another. The tubers grown with manure were superior. The party were then driven in two brakes to the farm of Treaton, tenanted by Mr Fyshe. They were taken to a large field planted with Farmer's Glory. Potatoes were dug up in different parts, and the opinions were "a very good show," "very bonnie," "very fine," and "very good, indeed." Twelve tubers were attached to some of the roots. Mr Fyshe stated that they had been raised by ordinary cultivation. Specimens of Maincrop showed that they were a good lot, while Goodhope was declared to be by one of those present "the best cooking potato he had had." The samples were good and numerous. Up-to-Date were dug up in another part of the field, and were declared to be "a splendid crop." Twelve and thirteen big potatoes were sometimes attached to the roots. The concensus of opinion appeared to be that this potato, for all-round superiority, was the best that had been shown.

Exhibition of Mr Findlay's Potatoes at Markinch.

(From the *Fife Herald and Journal* of 3rd October, and *Fife News* of 6th October, 1894.)

Mr Findlay, Markinch, the well-known potato rearer, held his annual field exhibition on Saturday under the most favourable weather. Mr Findlay had arranged for getting the fast train leaving Edinburgh at 9.35 to stop for the occasion at Markinch, and it brought a large contingent of gentlemen interested in the day's proceedings—including three who had come all the way from over the Border. The party proceeded to a small field close to the station, where a start was made. The first variety to be unearthed was Farmer's Glory, a potato which, from its productiveness and disease-resisting qualities, has come well to the front. Several shaws were dug, and showed from eight to a dozen sound marketable tubers, of a fine shape, and absolutely free from any kind of taint. The results looked for were not, of course, such as were obtained in such a favourable potato season as last year; but the expressions on all sides were those of hearty approval. Mr Findlay next drove his graip into the roots of a coloured variety not yet named, and here again the result gave every satisfaction. Mr Findlay was, as usual, subjected to a good deal of "heckling." One interrogator asked why white potatoes always sold better than coloured ones? In reply, Mr Findlay said he thought it arose from a dread or prejudice against disease—the colour remaining even after the potato was dressed, and giving rise to suspicions. A shaw of one of the second earlies was not a whit behind the others in point of quality; but, as Mr Findlay remarked, it was out of the question to look for a large crop in such a season. The produce of a shaw of the British Queen was pronounced "a fair sample of potatoes, with wonderful immunity from disease." Mr Findlay also mentioned that the field in which these samples were growing had only been got by him in the spring, and that previous to that it had not been manured for thirty years. The party thereafter adjourned to the residence of their host, where cake and wine were partaken of before beginning the day's work proper.

Several varieties of Mr Findlay's new earlies were handed round for inspection. These included Ladas, Aurora, Snowdrift, Challenge, Ruby Queen, Lady Rosabelle, Exhibitor, and British Queen, and all came in for more or less favourable criticism from the experts present.

After lunch, Mr Findlay led his party to a garden where potatoes are being raised from the seed of the apple, and where various applications of manure are being tested. There he dug up a couple of roots grown from the seed, and both showed abundance of tubers; but, as was only to be expected, they were very small in size. Crossing the road, another garden was entered, where samples of the Exhibitor were grown in two plots under different conditions. In the first, where silicate was used, the potatoes were pronounced good; but in the second plot, where the ordinary garden manure was used, the tubers were splendid, and Mr Fyshe exclaimed—"If these are a fair sample, ye may say guid-bye to your silicate." Professor Hunter also ridiculed the idea of people expecting to grow potatoes from glass—silicate being largely composed of that material.

The party again retraced their steps into the town, where machines were in waiting to convey them to Mr Fyshe's farm of Treaton. After a pleasant drive of a few miles, the farm was reached, and its tidy appearance at once commended itself to the English visitors, who expressed their determination to have a "look through" before leaving. During a short walk to the scene of operations, conversation again turned on the merits or demerits of silicate. Mr Findlay said if it had a merit at all it was that it seemed to harden up the plants. In answer to one of the party, he stated that he did not approve of basic slag for potatoes or anything of that nature. He had tried it, and found that it was of no use to him.

On arrival in the field, several shaws of Farmer's Glory were dug up, and showed an average of a dozen marketable potatoes—the last one producing fifteen. Maincrops, though scarcely so prolific, were all of excellent quality. Perhaps most interest, however, centered round the variety which gave so much promise last year, and which was then christened Goodhope. The roots which were turned up fully justified the name given to the variety, and Mr Findlay remarked that this was about the best keeping potato he had. Another of Mr Findlay's new maincrop potatoes, Up-to-Date, showed splendid results, and won the admiration of those present. Some of the tubers were round and others kidney-shaped; but all were noted for cleanness and healthiness. Mr Fyshe pointed out that the ground had only received the ordinary agricultural treatment. The upper part of the field was also visited; but though the crop here was scarcely so productive as that on the lower part, it was sufficiently good to win the hearty commendations of those whose opinion was worth having.

The exhibition over, the party had a look through Mr Fyshe's well-kept steading, and admired his stock, especially the pigs. The brakes were soon re-entered, and the party were driven to the Bethune Arms Hotel, where Mr Kinnes had an excellent repast provided, including a number of the potatoes which had been dug in the morning. These had all been carefully kept separate in the cooking, so that those at the table had an opportunity of sampling the various kinds. All were pronounced excellent; but the concensus of opinion seemed to be in favour of the Up-to-Date variety, which, it was stated, promised well to rival the famous Bruce.

Exhibition of Potatoes at Markinch.

(From the *Dundee Courier* of 1st October, and *Dundee Weekly News* of 6th October, 1894.)

Mr Archibald Findlay, Markinch, the successful propagator of The Bruce and other famous varieties of potatoes, continues his efforts in the production of new sorts, which give promise of successful results. The annual exhibition of Mr Findlay's various new varieties took place at Markinch on Saturday, when a large number of gentlemen interested in agriculture, and specially in the production of potatoes, attended. On the arrival of the most of the company by the Glasgow fast train, which was timed to stop for the convenience of the visitors at Markinch, those present at once proceeded to a small field adjoining the railway station, where a beginning was made. The first variety to be graiped was that of Farmer's Glory, which has been giving signs of a prolific cropper and of disease-resisting tubers. The shaw, on being turned out, showed eight pretty marketable tubers and three seconds. Other shaws were dug, when as many as ten and a dozen of fine-looking tubers were produced. These were much admired for their fine shape, and there was no appearance of a taint.

In answer to a question, Mr Findlay said the ground had only got a little manure, and it had been very much run out before it came into his possession last year. The crop in the circumstances was really fine, and this new variety is sure to become a favourite. Several shaws of a variety of coloured potatoes not yet named were then dug, which showed a large produce. Another new variety, named the British Queen, was afterwards shown. The first shaw unearthed produced some splendid tubers, and a sufficient number were dug to admit of their cooking quality being proved at the dinner to be held in the afternoon. An adjournment was then made to Mr Findlay's residence for lunch, at the close of which a large number of letters of apology from gentlemen unable to be present were read, among the number being Mr John Gilmour of Montrave; Mr John Loescher, Stockland Farm, near Birmingham; Mr David Inglis, manager for Earl Grey, Northumberland; Mr Charles Whitehead, Barming House, Maidstone; Mr James Stenhouse, Turnhouse, Cramond, &c. Before leaving the house the visitors were shown a selection of Mr Findlay's most popular new varieties, among which were Challenge, Snowdrift, Eightyfold, Ruby Queen, Lady Rosabelle, &c., which will shortly be put in the market. These had every appearance of good quality. The visitors were subsequently conducted to one of Mr Findlay's gardens, where a number of shaws were turned out, being the produce of the plum. In an adjoining garden several patches of the Exhibitor, which are to be on Mr Findlay's selling list this year, were examined. On the first patch, which was manured with silicate, the shaws dug showed fairly good production, the tubers being of a fine, round, medium size. These, however, were fairly eclipsed on the portion of the ground to which ordinary farmyard manure had been applied, several of the shaws having over a dozen each of large, fine potatoes. This result proved very gratifying to those of the visitors who do not approve of artificial manure. The company were then conveyed in a large brake and a machine to the farm of Treaton, tenanted by Mr James Fyshe, who has been of valuable assistance to Mr Findlay in conducting his operations and experiments in the propagation of his tubers. Beginning first with a portion of Mr Fyshe's crop, a shaw or two of the Farmer's Glory was dug up. These showed a most bounteous crop, as upwards of a dozen of fine tubers were found at each root. In the last as many as fifteen marketable potatoes were found. Continuing on Mr Fyshe's own planting, a large section of Maincrops were visited. These were found to be of very fine quality, though scarcely so productive as some of the other varieties, but sufficient to make the crop a very remunerative one to Mr Fyshe. The company then proceeded to a portion of the field sub-tenanted by Mr Findlay. A few shaws of Exhibitor were unearthed, but here they were found to be scarcely so numerous as at the formerly mentioned. The next lot to be graiped were last year named Goodhope. This variety gave excellent promise in its experimental stage, and the title given it was thought very appropriate. The first shaw revealed ten excellent marketable tubers without any small. Successive shaws were tried, and turned out from eight to ten tubers. These were much admired. Mr Findlay remarked that he was of opinion that they would be among the best keeping potatoes he had. The last variety to which attention was given was that of Up-to-Date, of which Mr Findlay has a large quantity to put on the market this year. The cropping of them last year proved most abundant. They are fine-looking potatoes, something like Sutton's Abundance. The ground was in excellent condition, and the prognostications as to success were highly borne out by the results of the magnificent crop displayed. The first shaw graiped produced ten marketable tubers and a few seconds, the next turned out a dozen, and the following one thirteen. In answer to a query, Mr Fyshe said the land was treated to the ordinary rule of agriculture in the district. Several other shaws were unearthed, all of which bore evidence of a most prolific crop, in one of which there were no fewer than sixteen fine marketable tubers. The whole of the gentlemen expressed their delight and satisfaction at the excellent results they had seen of this fine variety, which it was thought would be sure to become a favourite, and even rival the famous Bruce. This having concluded the exhibition, the visitors were soon again reseated, and the party were then driven to Markinch, where in the Bethune Arms Inn they were entertained to dinner.

New Markinch Potatoes.

(From the *N. B. Agriculturist* of 20th September, 1893.)

"Fareweel Scotland, I'm awa tae Fife." Such were our sentiments on Monday last, when, having fought our way through a crowd of Edinburgh holiday-makers, we found ourselves in the north-going train bound for Mr Findlay's annual potato picnic. A smart run through the well cleared fields, and by the already snugly thatched stackyards of the "Kingdom," brought us to Markinch, where we received a hearty welcome from Mr Findlay, and joined a company of about thirty gentlemen interested in potato-raising, who had come together in response to a special invitation, to inspect the new sorts to be brought out during the coming season. Among those present were the following:—Mr Peter Fyshe, Newtonlees; Mr Alexander Hope, East Barns; Mr John Inglis of Colluthie; Mr R. Inglis, Blinkbonny; Mr Dun, Kincaple, secretary of Fife Farmers' Club; Mr Cooper, Melling, Liverpool; Mr Braid, Abercrombie; Mr James Bayne, Muirhead; Mr Melville, Rumdewan; Mr Lamb, Stranton Grange, West Hartlepool; Mr Willian, Shincliffe Hall, Durham; Mr Bowie, Dunbar; Mr Inglis, Howick Hall; Mr Page, Myregornie; Mr Marshall, Dundee; Mr George Innes, *Fife Herald*; Mr R. K. Anderson, *N. B. Agriculturist*, &c., &c.

Letters of apology for absence were sent by Captain Gilmour of Montrave; Mr P. Hunter of Waterybutts; Mr Andrew Hutcheson, Dundee; Mr R. Sinclair-Scott of Craigievar; Mr M'Jannet, Over-Inzievar; Messrs James Carter & Co., of London; and Mr James Macdonald, secretary of the Highland Society, besides a large number of potato growers throughout the kingdom.

As to Mr Findlay's work in the selecting and hybridising of the best types of potatoes, by collecting the pollen of the one and fertilising it with the blossom of the other, little need be said, as it has been so frequently described in these columns; but from the specimens put before the company on Monday, there was little room to doubt that he has been remarkably successful in raising new sorts which possess robustness of constitution, great productiveness, and solidity, combined with good flavour. Self-educated, and naturally gifted with a taste for scientific pursuits, together with an indomitable spirit of perseverance, Mr Findlay seems to have acquired that habit of painstaking attention to detail which has in latter life done him such good service. This quality is absolutely necessary for successful potato-raising, and, together with the intuitive knowledge of "how to mate," its possession has placed Mr Findlay in the position of the most successful potato-raiser of the present time, and won for him the lasting gratitude of agriculturists, not only throughout Great Britain and Ireland, but in all parts of the world.

Mr Findlay's house was the first rendezvous, where light refreshments were served. Attention was here drawn to a very choice collection of specimens of this year's novelties taken from his garden trial plots, amongst which we select for mention (1) Ruby Queen, a flattish, purple, round, rough-coated sort, possessing excellent table qualities, whose appearance was warmly commended by many present; (2) Snowdrift, considered by Mr Findlay to be the finest white round potato he has yet produced; (3) Challenge, a kind that grew 30 lbs. of good sound potatoes on 9½ feet of a 24-inch drill; and (4) Aurora, a very hardy-looking hybrid out of the old Blue Don.

These being duly inspected and admired, the party set out in the waggonettes provided by their good host for

PITILLOCK

(Mr M'Gregor's), about two miles distant, where, on a slope over 450 feet above sea-level, Mr Findlay has a large number of drills grown unmanured, and close planted to keep down the size for seeding purposes. Here the serious work of the day began, Mr Fyshe, Newtonlees, acting as demonstrator, and giving the results of the plants examined. Unfortunately, owing to the exceptional dryness of the season, the tubers inspected were not seen to best advantage, for, excepting the "second early" varieties, none had attained the size they would have done in a season of average moisture. The first "graiped" was an unnamed late-ripening maincrop kidney, three stems yielding forty-three marketable potatoes and a fair proportion of seed.

Mr Findlay then led the way to another drill, where one of the "clinkers" of the season, a cross of the old Victoria with the Blue Don, called the Up-to-Date, was carefully examined, and when three stalks had been duly uprooted it was found that the total yield was thirty-three good potatoes and fourteen smalls. The tubers are large and of fine quality, and have every appearance of heavy cropping. Another new kind inspected in the same field was Lady Rosabelle, so called because Mr Findlay was deep in the poetry of the immortal Sir Walter when he discovered its value among his plots. It is of moderate size, flattish round shape, and roughish skin; when boiled and served it is the perfection of a table potato, being mealy, white, and of exceptionally good flavour. Yet another novelty was found in this field in Farmer's Glory, a late sort, of which three stems yielded thirty-three good and ten seed potatoes; it is a very large solid potato, and if it had had rain would have been seen to much better advantage. At the end of the day some large growers pronounced it the best thing they had seen during the day.

MUIRHEAD.

Leaving the slopes of Pitillock, the party was next conducted to Muirhead, tenanted by Mr Bayne, who had the honour of first growing The Bruce as a field crop, and here they made an interesting examination of a new kidney seedling. The haulms appeared good and strong, and on being tested thirty-five good sized potatoes were found on three stems, with five "smalls" in addition. As this prolific cropper had not received a name, Mr Findlay proposed to call it the Mr Hope, in honour of Mr Hope of East Barns, our largest East Lothian grower, but as some of the company pointed out that one word would be more convenient for commercial purposes, it was decided, on the suggestion of Mr Fyshe, to christen the newcomer Goodhope, and thus meet the wishes of all.

CARRISTON.

Mounting the brakes again, the party drove through the crofting village of Star, in the schoolhouse of which Annie Swan wrote the "Gates of Eden," and came to Carriston, where they were most hospitably entertained by the genial laird, Mr Thomas Lawson. Although the soil at Carriston is mossy and sandy, and quite unsuitable for potato cultivation, still the party saw some grand crops in the field of The Bruce, Farmer's Glory, Maincrop, Her Majesty, and Sutton's Abundance, all furrowed up by Messrs Newland & Son's (Linlithgow) ridging plough, reckoned by Mr Lawson to be one of the most serviceable implements for this operation. The sight of the day, however, was found in Mr Lawson's garden, where two stems of Farmer's Glory, grown three feet apart (each way), manured with the equivalent of twelve loads of farmyard manure per acre, gave the astounding result as follows:—No. 1 stem, twenty-seven well-developed potatoes, weighing 14 lbs.; No. 2 stem, twenty-nine potatoes, weighing $14\frac{1}{4}$ lbs. This works out as equal to a yield of 30 tons 6 cwts. per acre, and if this result can be extended to field cultivation—and we see no reason why it should not be—this potato is one with a future before it. A stem of the Goodhope kind, grown under the same conditions in the garden, gave twenty-one well-developed tubers. After a "refresher" at Carriston, the last place visited was

TREATON,

tenanted by Mr Fyshe, J.P. Here the party dismounted, and proceeded to a field where they had the opportunity of seeing Up-to-Date grown under more favourable conditions than at Pitillock; its strong and upright haulms were much admired, and a few stems taken at random gave the following results—7, 8, 14, 22, 28 potatoes each. It appears to be a good disease resister, and possesses the qualities requisite for a good practical marketable potato. The field inspection having concluded, the party drove back to the Bethune Arms Hotel, where they were most hospitably entertained to dinner by Mr Findlay, and the potatoes inspected were served up boiled in their "jackets," so that the company had also the opportunity of judging their table merits. Mr Fyshe, of Newtonlees, acted as chairman, and Mr Dun, of Kincaple, as croupier.

Practice with Science.

POTATO PROPAGATION IN FIFESHIRE.

(From *Mark Lane Express* and *Agricultural Journal*, 25th September, 1893.)

A large and distinguished party of visitors last week witnessed the results of the present season's work in improving potato culture, which has been carried out for some years in Fifeshire by Mr Archibald Findlay, Markinch, who has been giving his undivided attention to the propagation of potatoes, and has been very successful. The success of The Bruce variety is one of Mr Findlay's earliest triumphs. Though only eight years since it was placed in the market it is already known not only in all the potato-growing counties in the United Kingdom, but in some of our colonies. Among the other successful varieties which Mr Findlay has produced are Jeanie Deans, Thane o' Fife, Lady Frances, Her Majesty, and many others, which are making their way steadily into favour, and he has a large number of new varieties at various stages of development which also give promise of successful results. A field of about seventeen acres is rented by Mr Findlay for the growing of his seed potatoes, the soil of which is of a comparatively light nature, but is very suitable for Mr Findlay's purpose. In answer to inquiries by a number of the inspecting party, Mr Findlay explained that he used for the purpose of the development of his seed no farmyard manure, as his object was not the production of heavy crops, but that of tubers of fine quality and good appearance. They had only had a light dressing of artificial manure, of which dissolved bones was the principal constituent. He had always adopted the principle of planting from fairly full-sized seed planted whole, as he found that, other things being equal, he got a better yield than from small-sized or cut tubers. The first of Mr Findlay's new varieties to be dug up was a shaw, No. 23, not yet named. It was a good-looking kidney-shaped potato, and had the appearance of a good resister. It turned out seven fine marketable tubers and a goodly number of seconds. Three shaws of a variety of kidney were then graiped, the produce of which delighted the onlookers. In the first was found twelve marketable tubers and two seconds, the second had nine of the former and three of the latter, while the third produced nine of the former. These potatoes were of fine quality, and greatly pleased the company. They are three years old only, and give excellent promise of turning out very successfully. Proceeding to the portion of the field where the new variety of Up-to-Date, which is a four-year old, and of which excellent results were last year anticipated, the expectations of the visitors were raised to a high pitch. Three shaws were laid bare, which showed the largest yield which had yet been seen. The first produced twelve pretty tubers fit for table use, and five seconds, the second ten and one, and the third eleven and eight respectively. Mr Findlay was highly complimented for these extra results, and, in answer to a question as to its propagation, he said it was a cross between the old Victoria and a seedling of the old Blue Don. They were planted, he said, in the last days of the month of April. In other parts of the field various shaws of the same variety were also dug with like gratifying results. The variety of Farmer's Glory was then exhibited. Mr Findlay stated that the want of rain had been very much against the growth of the tubers. The first shaw graiped showed the bulkiest crop come across up to that time, the produce being no less than thirteen good potatoes and five seconds. Other two shaws showed like gratifying results. Specimens of Her Majesty were next shown. In the first there was one bearing traces of the disease. In the other shaws no taint was found, and the crop was found to be very abundant.

The party then visited the farm at Muirhead tenanted by Mr Bayne. The only variety grown here was an unnamed seedling new kidney. A number of shaws were at once here turned up, and the crop was immense, ten and a dozen large tubers being found at each, with fully a half-dozen seconds also at each. The company again entered the conveyances, and, after a smart run of fully three miles, they were greeted at Carriston by the laird, Mr Lawson, who has been an able coadjutor of Mr Findlay in his difficult work. Maincrop, Jeanie Deans, and Farmer's Glory were tried. The two former showed a fairly good crop, but the latter, as at Pitillock, was extremely heavy, and very promising attractive tubers. Lady Frances, of which high hopes were raised last year, was found to be yielding a large crop. Four shaws of the famous Bruce were turned up, the produce of which showed fifty-two marketable tubers and about twenty seconds. Her Majesty was found to be very prolific, two shaws producing thirty-one firsts and five seconds free from any taint. A visit was then paid to Carriston garden, where several of the varieties had been planted, and had received special care, and had been planted one yard apart. The first shaw turned up was of Farmer's Glory, the produce of which was most extraordinary, resulting in twenty-seven large tubers, which, on being weighed, turned the scale at 14 lbs. A neighbouring shaw of the same variety turned out twenty-nine tubers, and weighed 14¼ lbs. Such a yield was considered extraordinary. A shaw of No. 3, which had been treated in the same manner, was found to have twenty-one good-sized tubers, weighing 10 lbs. The journey was then resumed, the farm of Mr James Fyshe, Treaton, about two miles distant, being the next halt, and where a good quantity of Up-to-Date have this year been grown. Here the most extraordinary results had been attained. The ground was in excellent condition, and the tubers, which have the shape of Sutton's Abundance, left nothing further to be desired either in abundance or quality. The yield of a number of shaws varied from ten to twenty fine potatoes, and in some cases with the addition of a number of seconds. A very high opinion of this variety was formed, and it is expected to rival The Bruce.

Potato Propagation.

(From *The Farmer and Stockbreeder and Chamber of Agriculture Journal*,
25th September, 1893.)

In the propagation of new varieties of potatoes perhaps no one individual has accomplished more genuinely useful work than has Mr Archibald Findlay, Markinch, Fifeshire, N.B. For many years Mr Findlay has been giving his undivided attention to the propagation of potatoes, and has been very successful. The success of The Bruce variety is one of Mr Findlay's earliest triumphs. Though only eight years since it was placed on the market it is already known not only in all the potato-growing counties in the United Kingdom but in some of our colonies. Among the other successful varieties which Mr Findlay has produced are Jeanie Deans, Thane o' Fife, Lady Frances, Her Majesty, and many others which are making their way steadily into favour, and he has a large number of new varieties, such as Up-to-Date, Farmer's Glory, Goodhope, and others, at various stages of development, which also give promise of successful results.

New Varieties of Potatoes.

(From the *Farming World* of 6th October, 1893.)

In last issue something was said of the risky and speculative character of the potato crop. It was pointed out that much of the risk which the growing of potatoes involves is due to the liability of the crop to injury from disease. That liability is intensified by a strong tendency in all varieties of potatoes to lose vitality under continued cultivation.

Some varieties degenerate quickly, rising rapidly into favour because of their high quality and prolific character, and losing popularity just as quickly through their inability to resist the attacks of disease. Their constitution would, so to speak, seem to be weak, and so they soon fall a prey to fungoid enemies.

In other varieties there is greater stamina, a constitution of greater robustness. These varieties longer resist the tendency to degenerate, and are therefore not so liable to be destroyed by disease. A most notable instance of this is the well-known Champion, which has so long held a high place amongst varieties largely cultivated.

Even the Champion, however, is showing signs of a weakening constitution, thus strengthening the belief that there is a natural tendency in all cultivated varieties of plants—aye, and of animals too—to decline in constitutional vigour. No doubt, by liberal and judicious treatment, this tendency to degenerate may be to some extent counteracted. Skilful farmers have done, and are doing this with marked success, both in the case of animals and plants. Sooner or later, however, there comes a day when old varieties succumb.

In view of these facts, it is surely a matter of great importance that attention should be given to the raising of new varieties to take the place of those that disappear. This remark applies to all farm crops, but has a particular application to the potato crop. It is generally acknowledged that one of the most practicable and effective methods of combating potato disease is the raising of new varieties of robust constitution. Much has been done in this way to lessen the farmer's loss from the *Peronaspora infestans*. And there is room and need for still more work of a similar kind.

It is for these reasons that we have taken special pleasure in from time to time directing public attention to the splendid work in which Mr A. Findlay, Markinch, Fifeshire, has been engaged. Mr Findlay is a most enthusiastic propagator of new varieties of potatoes. He has given much time and attention to the work, and has been highly successful. His name has become widely known in association with those excellent new varieties The Bruce, Her Majesty, Jeanie Deans, and others, and he is still busy as ever raising up new varieties of the popular esculent.

The inspection of Mr Findlay's potato trials has become quite an annual event in agricultural circles. As noticed three issues ago, it was held this year on the 18th September, and was well attended by farmers. The varieties already named are growing excellent crops, and so are several other newer sorts which have not yet been given to the public.

The Farmer's Glory is evidently to be a very prolific cropper. From two stems of this variety there were gathered no fewer than fifty-six tubers, giving a gross weight of no less than 29½ lbs. We trust Mr Findlay will be encouraged to continue his splendid work, which cannot fail to be of much value to his brother farmers.

A Great Field Day at Markinch.

ANNUAL EXHIBITION OF MR FINDLAY'S POTATOES.

(From the *Fife Herald and Journal* of 20th September, 1893.)

The natives of world-famous Markinch were somewhat puzzled and bewildered on Monday by an unusual influx of strangers. Some of the visitors came by rail from the North, and some from the South, others by ordinary vehicle, and the residue by that most ancient and safest form of all locomotion—"shanks-nagie." Not only did they hail from both sides of the Forth, but England itself sent forward an honourable deputation—a fact which the picturesque blending of the purest Cockney with the "braidest" Scotch must have made patent to the most casual bystander. The company, it may here be mentioned, was specially interested in an important branch of agriculture—potato-growing—and its representative character may be gathered from the following list of names:—Mr Peter Fyshe, Newtonlees, Dunbar; Mr Bowe, sen., Dunbar; Mr Bowe, jun., Dunbar; Mr Sporl, Lancashire; Mr

Stranfin, Durham; Mr Willian, Shincliffe, Durham; Mr Cooper, Melling, Liverpool; Mr Lamb, West Hartlepool; Mr Alexander Hope, jun., East Barns, Dunbar; Mr Inglis of Colluthie, Cupar; Mr R. Inglis, Blinkbonny, Cupar; Mr Inglis (manager for Earl Grey), Howick Gardens, Northumberland; Mr Braid, Abercrombie; Mr George Dun, Easter Kincaple, St Andrews; Mr Melville, Rumdewan, Kettle; Mr Bayne, Muirhead; Mr Westwood, sen., Cupar; Mr Innes, *Fife Herald and Journal*, Cupar; Mr William Taylor, Leslie; Mr R. Anderson, *N. B. Agriculturist*; Mr Marshall, produce-broker, Dundee; Mr Page, Myregornie, Markinch; &c.

A circular issued by Mr A. Findlay, Portland House, Markinch—the well-known raiser of The Bruce—was the talisman that brought this widely scattered band together, said circular announcing Mr Findlay's intention to submit for the company's inspection "several new and very promising varieties of potatoes, which had now passed the experimental stage." Preparatory to setting out for the fields in which these objects of interest were to be found, cake and wine were served in Mr Findlay's dining-room, and among a number of apologies on the table from agriculturists in all parts of the country, one was observed from Mr Gilmour of Montrave, who, dating from Black Corries, Ballachulish, wrote that his absence from the county was his only excuse for not availing himself of "an opportunity of seeing what was of great practical interest." On a side table stood several specimens of "Findlay's new early potatoes for season 1894," the most noteworthy of which was probably the Challenge—a second early somewhat similar in shape to the Abundance. Of this Challenge variety, Mr Findlay said it had lowered the record of all his former experiences. Under ordinary cultivation he had grown 30 lbs. of it, all fit for table use, on $9\frac{1}{3}$ feet of a 24-inch drill—a rate of produce equal, according to table 7 in Balfour's Farmers' Account Book, to 30 tons 16 cwts. per acre!

All having been got ready for the start, a cavalcade, comprising a large brake, a waggonette, and a dog-cart, set out for the farm of Pitillock, where, as last year, Mr Findlay has a large breadth set apart in two fields for the growing of his seed potatoes. Conversation in the brake naturally turned on the state of the green crops in the different districts to which the visitors belonged, and the urgent need south of the Forth, and indeed everywhere, for rain.

Descending at field No. 1 on Pitillock, Mr Findlay explained that all his seed was grown by artificial manure, and that he believed in planting *whole* seed instead of cut. He then plunged his "graip" into the stems of an unnamed kidney. Three such diggings brought out the very respectable average of $14\frac{1}{3}$ potatoes to each shaw. All were entirely free of disease, and in appearance and quality met with cordial approval. The averages of two other similar series of three graipings were fourteen and thirteen. In field No. 2 special interest was manifested in Mr Findlay's new variety Up-to-Date, a four-year old that begun last year to attract some attention. The first shaw dug up revealed no fewer than seventeen tubers at the roots. Other two graipings made the average over the whole $15\frac{2}{3}$ potatoes—a fact that spoke for itself of the variety's productiveness. Further digging at Pitillock was also regarded as highly satisfactory. Farmer's Glory was likewise tested, eighteen potatoes being found at the root of the first shaw. Specimens of Her Majesty were next shown. In the first there was one bearing traces of disease; but in the others no taint was found, and the produce was very plentiful.

A short run from Pitillock brought the company to Muirhead, tenanted by Mr Bayne. One or two unnamed seedlings were unearthed here—the most notable of which, in point of quantity and quality, was then and there christened Goodhope. The conveyances were again set in motion, and after an enjoyable three miles' drive *via* Balbirnie Home Farm, the inspecting party were landed at Carriston steading, where the genial laird and occupant, Mr Lawson, gave every one a cordial welcome. Proceeding to a field but a few steps from the "toon," little time was lost in diving into the *root* of the matter, for Mr Lawson has long been an invaluable fellow-worker with Mr Findlay in the interesting domain of potato culture. The field in which the company found themselves was in excellent condition. A crop of oats was taken off last year; but, previous to that, the ground had lain thirty years in pasture. The management also elicited high commendation. Not only was every drill as clean as a ribbon, but the furring up was simply perfection. In a conspicuously large and bulky crop, not a green tuber was to be seen. The varieties tested were:—Maincrop, Jeanie Deans, Farmer's Glory, Lady Frances, Bruce, and Her Majesty, and in every instance, almost without exception, the results were most satisfactory. Two shaws of Her Majesty yielded thirty-six potatoes between them, and The Bruces, which gave fifty-two marketable potatoes and twenty seconds for four shaws, were reckoned to be yielding at least 12 tons the acre. Mr Lawson had still bigger things in store. Conducting the wanderers through a charmingly laid-out parterre, in which begonias and calceolarias were in gorgeous bloom, he called a halt at a testing plot in his kitchen garden. Here several sorts were planted, after what might be termed the draught-board pattern—that is to say, that to each seed was allotted an exact square yard. Farmer's Glory was the first turned up. Two shaws were dug, and the result in each case was a staggerer. There were twenty-seven splendid potatoes at the one shaw, and twenty-nine at the other. They weighed 14 and $14\frac{1}{4}$ lbs. respectively, being at the rate of 30 tons 5 cwts., and 30 tons 16 cwts. per acre—a sufficiently significant tribute to the possibilities of good seed and high cultivation. A brief but refreshing sojourn under Mr Lawson's hospitable roof-tree terminated the visit to his interesting homestead; and again our cicerone hurried us on to yet another scene of victory. The field in this last instance was on the farm of Treaton, tenanted by Mr James Fyshe, a brother of Mr Fyshe of Newtonlees, and a recently-appointed J.P. On the field at Treaton the variety inspected was Up-to-Date, and the results obtained only confirmed the very favourable opinions already formed of its merits. This field was also in excellent condition, and, with the adjoining breadth of beautiful purple-topped Swedes, spoke for itself of Mr Fyshe's intelligent farming.

Returning to Markinch, the party were entertained by Mr Findlay to a capital dinner in the Bethune Arms. Mr Fyshe, Newtonlees, occupied the chair, and Mr Dun, Easter Kincaple, acted as croupier. In proposing the toast of the evening—"Mr Findlay's health and success"—the Chairman spoke in cordial terms of the services rendered agriculture by Mr Findlay's indomitable energy and enthusiasm in the raising of new potatoes. He predicted a bright future for Up-to-Date, and suggested that Mr Findlay should next introduce a variety that would enable tenants to "buy up their landlords." (Laughter and applause.) Mr Findlay, in replying, expressed his appreciation of the patronage that had all along been bestowed upon him, a patronage that was increasing year by year. He specially thanked those friends who had come all the way from England to see his exhibition. Mr Lamb, West Hartlepool, said he had been a grower of potatoes all his life, and had bought The Bruce from Mr Findlay, with the result that it was the best cropper he had. He planted good-sized seed. Mr Cooper, Melling, Liverpool, said he had tried four or five of Mr Findlay's varieties, and they had all proved extraordinary croppers with very little disease. What he had sent out last spring had also given every satisfaction. The Lady Frances in particular seemed to suit his part of the country, where they went in for vegetable gardening; but they all did well, and, with large seeds, produced from 20 to 30 tons per Cheshire acre.

Disease-Resisting Potatoes.

(From the *Horticultural Times* of 4th March, 1893.)

The importance of an extended production of the tuber amongst fruit and market garden growers in this country has been dealt with by us again and again, hence we are pleased to draw attention to the disease-resisting potatoes which for some years Mr A. Findlay, the famous seed-grower of Markinch, N.B., has popularised, especially with the Scottish and northern agriculturists. Mr Findlay has done so much for the production of new varieties of potatoes, which are not only distinguished as heavy croppers, but are noted for their disease-resisting qualities as well, that a notice of his specialities deserves consideration.

As the outcome of an experiment conducted at the Munster Dairy and Agricultural School, the famous Bruce, a variety originally raised by Mr Findlay, not only produced the heaviest crop of all the varieties experimented with, but also proved absolutely free from disease; while all the other leading varieties grown in that experiment were more or less—and some of them notably so—tainted with disease. A great deal is being written just now as to the partial success in some instances of the sulphate of copper remedy against potato disease; but it will be remembered that last year the extensive experiments with this remedy, which were carried out by the Highland Society of Scotland and the Royal Dublin Society, served to show that the treatment was ineffectual to prevent the spread of the disease. The best and most effectual remedy against the disease, therefore, must be to plant only robust varieties of potatoes, which are known to be practically proof against disease, and of these The Bruce is an outstanding example. But The Bruce is not the only great success that Mr Findlay has scored, and some of his newer varieties give promise of even outrivalling his first success. Special interest, therefore, must attach to the annual public examination of all the new varieties of potatoes grown by him for seed purposes. Our readers will remember that the *Horticultural Times* was the only trade journal in London which maintained the views demonstrated by the two above-mentioned societies, and we are glad to see the conclusions of such an eminently practical authority as Mr Findlay in agreement with our views. Another point Mr Findlay settles beyond dispute, which we heartily endorse. We refer to the question of "whole" *versus* "cut" seed potatoes. The question as to whether potato seed should be cut or planted whole has often been disputed. Both theories have numerous followers. Mr A. Findlay advocates the use of whole seed. He maintains that the extra cost in seed is more than compensated for by a more vigorous plant, and a heavier yield of larger potatoes.

Mr Findlay has, perhaps, done more than any other man living to maintain and advance the potato-growing trade of this country—and foreign countries as well. For many years he has patiently and studiously prosecuted his favourite pursuit. Whatever may be the outcome of this attempt, he goes on year after year experimenting and developing seedlings, until he has commanded success to reward his exertions. Mr Findlay's is a most peculiar study. The amount of time and pains that he devotes to the propagation and production of new sorts of potatoes are surprising beyond all comprehension. When one hears of the universal popularity of The Bruce, and the rapidly rising fame of Her Majesty, Lady Frances, Jeanie Deans, and many other kinds, he inclines to the idea that the propagation of the potato knows no failure. Mr Findlay has quite a different story to relate. If, he says, he meets success once in every forty attempts, he considers himself fortunate. It often costs him more. In conclusion, we commend the admirable pamphlet Mr Findlay has just issued, because it deserves to be in the hands of every fruit and market garden grower in the country.

Some Facts on Potato Growing.

(From the *N. B. Agriculturist* of 19th October, 1892.)

We are all familiar with Dean Swift's axiom, to the effect that the man who makes two ears of corn or two blades of grass grow where only one grew before, is a genuine benefactor to his country. If this be true in regard to grain or grass, it must be equally true in regard to potatoes. Mr Findlay of Markinch, therefore, must be justly regarded as a benefactor to his country, seeing he has done so much for the production of new varieties of potatoes, which are not only distinguished as heavy croppers, but are noted for their disease-resisting qualities as well. Last week we quoted the facts respecting an experiment conducted at the Munster Dairy and Agricultural School, in which the famous Bruce, a variety originally raised by Mr Findlay, not only produced the heaviest crop of all the varieties experimented with, but also proved absolutely free from disease; while all the other leading varieties grown in that experiment were more or less—and some of them notably so—tainted with disease. A great deal is being written just now in some of the English papers as to the partial success in some instances of the sulphate of copper remedy against potato disease; but it will be remembered that last year the extensive experiments with this remedy, which were carried out by the Highland Society of Scotland, the "Royal" of England, and the Royal Dublin Society, served to show that this treatment was ineffectual to prevent the spread of the disease. The best and most effectual remedy against the disease, therefore, must be to plant only robust varieties of potatoes which are known to be practically proof against disease, and of these The Bruce is an outstanding example. But The Bruce is not the only great success that Mr Findlay has scored, and some of his newer varieties give promise of even outrivalling his first success. Special interest, therefore, must attach to the annual public examination of all the new varieties of potatoes grown by him for seed purposes. In connection with the report of this year's examination of his seed potato crops, which is given elsewhere, there is one important fact which falls to be noted. Mr Findlay has fully tested the productiveness of small-sized and cut seed as against full-sized seed planted whole, and he strongly holds that the best and heaviest crop is got by planting fairly full-sized seed uncut. In regard to this point, Mr Lawson of Carriston, who is an able and enthusiastic coadjutor of Mr Findlay's, calls our attention to an article communicated to the *New Zealand Farmer* by Mr David Dun, formerly of Mains of Kilconquhar, Fifeshire, and now of Greenhills, Gore, New Zealand. The Bruce, it appears, is as well known at the Antipodes as it is in its native country, and Mr Dun had made a careful experiment with The Bruce by way of testing the relative productiveness of small-sized and full-sized seed. The result was that the small-sized seed yielded a fairly good crop, but the egg-sized seed planted whole gave a much better crop, and the large-sized seed planted whole gave the heaviest crop of all. This experiment, therefore, by an old Fifeshire farmer at the Antipodes, fully confirms Mr Findlay's contention as to the superior advantages of planting good-sized seed whole in preference to using small-sized or cut seed.

The Bruce and its Rivals.

(From the *N. B. Agriculturist* of 19th October, 1892.)

On Thursday, a number of agriculturists who are deeply interested in potato-growing met at Markinch, on the invitation of Mr Findlay, potato seed grower, to examine the crops of new and disease-resisting varieties of potatoes which are being grown by him for seed purposes. Mr Findlay has done yeoman service to the country through the raising of new varieties of potatoes, which are not only disease-proof, but are also noted for their great productiveness; and The Bruce, which was one of the varieties raised by him, has now for several years held the proud position of absolute monarch in the potato field. Several of his new varieties, notably the Jeanie Deans, Lady Frances, and Thane o' Fife, are now pressing The Bruce rather hard in the contest for supremacy, and have won for Mr Findlay a unique reputation as a grower of seed potatoes. Instead, however, of resting on his well-won laurels, Mr Findlay continues to press steadily forward with the work of producing new varieties, and some of those which are to be brought out this season are promising to outrival not only in productiveness, but also in quality, any of the others he has previously produced. It was with the view of comparing the relative merits of these newer and older varieties of heavy-cropping and disease-resisting potatoes that the party met at Markinch on Thursday. Among others present were:—Mr Andrew Hutcheson, vice-chairman of the Perthshire County Council; Mr Cunningham, Dalachy; Mr Winton, Ardovie, Brechin; Mr Lawson, Carriston; Mr Fyshe, Treaton; Mr Melville, Ballomill; Mr Braid, Abercrombie; Mr Westwood, Cupar; Mr D. Young, *N. B. Agriculturist;* Mr Charles Macdonald, Edinburgh, &c. Letters expressing the deep regret of the writers at being unable to be present were also received from many prominent potato-growers throughout the country, including Mr James Hope, East Barns; Mr Peter Fyshe, Newtonlees, Dunbar; Mr Smith, Longniddry, &c.

The inspecting party first proceeded to Mr Findlay's garden, where a considerable number of new varieties raised from seedlings were being grown. Mr Findlay first of all gave a lucid explanation of the system of cross-fertilisation which he pursued, and showed how he "mated," so to speak, the one variety with the other, by shaking the pollen of the "sire" on the pistils of the "dam," and afterwards saving the "apples" for seed. The new varieties in the garden were all found to be still growing vigorously, their shaws being strong, fresh, and green. Mostly all gave promise of being exceedingly prolific, one of them showing eighteen marketable potatoes to the shaw, while another showed twenty, and each good-sized potato to the shaw is reckoned equal to one ton per acre. The productiveness of these new varieties was accentuated by the fact that the seedlings from which they were grown were only of the size of marbles.

The party next proceeded to the farm of Pitillock, where a field of eleven acres is all set apart for the growing of seed potatoes for Mr Findlay. The soil was of a comparatively light nature, but very suitable for this particular purpose. Mr Findlay explained that the potatoes in this field were all grown solely with a comparatively light dressing of artificial manure, of which dissolved bones formed the principal constituent, as his main object was not the production of abnormally heavy crops, but the production of tubers of very fine quality, with beautiful skins and a most attractive appearance. The number of potatoes at each shaw, therefore, would be much under what the same kind of potatoes would produce if more heavily manured. He also explained that the potatoes were all grown from fairly full-sized seed planted whole, as he found that potatoes of fairly full size planted whole always gave a much better yield than could be got—other things being equal—from smaller-sized or cut tubers. The first of the new varieties in this field to attract attention was Scottish Chief, a three-year old, of which a limited number will be for sale this year. This was a beautifully shaped potato, and it was certainly a very prolific one, each shaw dug up showing an average of a dozen marketable tubers. Another new variety which excited the enthusiastic admiration of all the visitors was Her Majesty, a potato whose attractive appearance and extreme productiveness argued a most successful reign for the new monarch. Most of the visitors were disposed to give Her Majesty the palm over all the other varieties. Three other new varieties—the one named Up-to-Date, and the others as yet known as No. 3 and No. 28—were greatly admired for their beautiful shapes and remarkable productiveness. Mr Findlay's earlier stocks of new varieties, including The Bruce, The Thane o' Fife, Lady Frances, and Jeanie Deans, were all found to be yielding an excellent crop, and were in every case perfectly free from disease.

The party then proceeded to Carriston, where Mr Lawson showed them a capital field of potatoes, in which some of the new varieties they had been inspecting at Pitillock were found growing. In this field both Her Majesty and Up-to-Date fully bore out the remarkable promise they had exhibited in the seed field, or nursery as it might rather be called, at Pitillock. The Jeanie Deans also met with much favour from the visitors, as also did the Lady Frances. A considerable part of the field was occupied by The Bruce, whose stamina and productiveness have been so fully proved on many a field. In this case, The Bruce showed an excellent crop, but which, as most of the visitors admitted, was scarcely equal to that yielded by Her Majesty, Up-to-Date, and No. 3. It may be remembered that at the complimentary dinner and presentation to Mr Findlay last year, Mr Lawson expressed the decided conviction that Her Majesty would soon be crowned as the monarch of the field, and his prediction seems in every way likely to be fully verified by the logic of events. Mr Lawson also took the visitors into his garden to see for themselves the harvesting of a single shaw of each of the different varieties of potatoes grown in the field. Each shaw had been grown from a good-sized potato planted whole, and each had got about three square feet of space, so as to give them the amplest freedom for growth and development. Under such conditions the number and weight of potatoes produced by each shaw was something enormous, but the great size of many of the tubers might have been against them in the eyes of buyers.

Proceeding next to Treaton, Mr Fyshe showed them a splendid field of potatoes, in which the principal varieties grown were The Bruce, Jeanie Deans, and Lady Frances. The crop was an uncommonly heavy one all over, and perfectly free from disease, and the visitors were loud in their praise of Mr Fyshe's skill and successful high farming, ample evidence of which was furnished by the plethoric condition of his stackyard, and the luxuriant fields of grain which had still to be gathered in.

The party then drove to the Bethune Arms Hotel, Markinch, where dinner had been provided for them by Mr Findlay. At the dinner, Mr Hutcheson occupied the chair, and Mr Lawson, Carriston, acted as croupier. The potatoes used at the dinner were samples of the Jeanie Deans and Lady Frances varieties, boiled in their "jackets," and the superb quality of both varieties was enthusiastically commented on by all the company.

Interesting Exhibition of Potatoes at Markinch.

(From the *Fife News* of 15th October, 1892.)

On the invitation of Mr A. Findlay, novelty potato grower, Markinch, a number of gentlemen visited that famous agricultural centre on Thursday for the purpose of inspecting his different varieties of potatoes. Those invited included representatives from Forfarshire, Perthshire, Fifeshire, and Midlothian, amongst whom were:—Messrs Lawson, Carriston; Hutcheson, vice-chairman, Perthshire County Council; Cunningham, Dalachy; Braid, Abercrombie; Winton, sen. and jun., Brechin; Melville, Kingskettle; Young, *N. B. Agriculturist;* Macdonald, *Farming World,* &c. The party assembling at Mr Findlay's house early in the day, proceeded to his garden, where a series of specimens were laid bare. The first potato "graiped" was an early seedling, two years planted, or three from the plum. The root yielded eighteen full-grown potatoes, all of which were considered of very good quality. The next tuber lifted was another seedling, kidney shaped. It yielded ten fine potatoes. Both seedlings, which have yet to be christened, were planted on the 18th of May, and were, to all appearance, excellent disease-resisters. Another shaw of seedlings (this year's) produced a nice pink and white coloured potato, not quite ripe. A remarkable feature of this variety is the tremendous amount of "wood" it carries. The first shaw of named varieties lifted was Up-to-Date. This is a beautiful, clean, kidney potato, and very prolific. The first shaw realised fourteen, and the second sixteen good marketable potatoes, which is at the rate of 15 tons per acre. These potatoes were entirely free from disease, and of a very high quality. The Bruce also came out well, and was the theme of considerable jocular remark. Mr Findlay then conducted his guests to another garden plot, where he put the graip in a likely shaw, and brought to the surface no less than forty-eight seed and ware and five small potatoes. A second early, they were of very fine quality, and a little later than Jeanie Deans. Another shaw was lifted in this plot, and also proved exceptionally good. The party then proceeded in a brake to the farm of Pitillock, where Mr Findlay rents from the tenant, Mr M'Gregor, a field of eleven acres, for the purpose of growing various kinds of seed potatoes. Mr Findlay, it may here be stated, does not use farmyard manure, finding that artificial treatment suits his purpose better. He also goes on the principle of planting his seed potatoes whole. The first potato lifted in the field was the Scottish Chief, a fine reddish-looking succulent. Lady Frances was very much admired, as was also Her Majesty, the latter being a very prolific potato. It seemed to be the general opinion that these two varieties would yet occupy a prominent position in the potato world. One of the shaws of Her Majesty yielded twenty-nine excellent marketable tubers. Thane o' Fife was shown in capital condition, and entirely free from disease. A small round potato was shown in Early Fortune. Another shaw of the same species was lifted, and the produce was found to be exceptionally large. Mr Findlay explained that the difference in size was due to the fact that the large potato had had much higher cultivation than the small. Another variety turned up, called No. 3, was described by Mr Findlay as, in his opinion, better than The Bruce. It is a nice kidney potato, and of the same family as Scottish Chief. Another lot of the same variety were shown in higher cultivation, and a marked difference was noticeable in the size. A root of Lady Frances was lifted, and pronounced of perfect shape and quality. A seedling of the Regent quality was very well shaped, and, according to Mr Findlay, is as hardy as The Bruce. Lady Rosabelle and Jeanie Deans were the only others lifted. The first-named, which was never known to have been touched with disease, was of very fine quality, while the latter was also a very clean-looking root. The inspection of this field over, Mr Lawson of Carriston's beautiful farm was next visited. Lady Fife, a nice, small, round potato, looked very well, and Nos. 2 and 3 bore favourable comparison with those shown on Mr Findlay's field. These two varieties very much resemble Beauty of Fife. Lady Frances also bore out its reputation here as being of a very prolific nature. Maincrop, which requires much better land than The Bruce, was a small crop. Her Majesty was in the pink of condition, and it was the opinion of those present that it had come best out of the test. A single seed of Bruce yielded twenty-three fine-looking potatoes. Mr Lawson then led the way to his garden, which was styled the "Carriston potato test ground." No. 2 was the first root lifted, and fifteen potatoes of enormous size met the view, while a root of Her Majesty realised twenty-four beauties. Among the others shown here were Parkhill Beauty, Jeanie Deans, and The Bruce. All these varieties were remarkable for their size. After the party had partaken of Mr Lawson's considerate hospitality, a visit was paid to the potato field of Mr Fyshe, Treaton. Lady Frances and Her Majesty were the principal varieties exhibited here. The former root showed a produce of no less than thirty-two potatoes.

At the conclusion of the inspection, Mr Findlay entertained his friends to a sumptuous dinner in the Bethune Arms. Mr Hutcheson occupied the chair, and Mr Lawson acted as croupier. In proposing "The Health of Mr Findlay," the Chairman said agriculturists all over the world were indebted to their host for the splendid strains of potatoes he had produced. He was of opinion that the varieties Her Majesty and Lady Frances were bound to come to the front, and he would advise those who had not grown them previously to go in for a quantity. Potatoes, like other things, seemed to weaken through time, and required an infusion of new blood. A good many of the old varieties had now died out. Regents were very liable to disease, and Champions and the old Perthshire Reds were now almost out of cultivation in this part of the country. He did not think those who had grown The Bruce had ever regretted doing so. Mr Hutcheson concluded by expressing the hope that Mr Findlay would be long spared to introduce many other varieties. Mr Findlay suitably replied, and thanked his friends for the popularity they had given to his earlier varieties of potatoes.

Whole *versus* Cut Seed Potatoes.

(From the *Farming World* of 21st October, 1892.)

The question as to whether potato seed should be cut or planted whole is somewhat disputed. Both theories have numerous followers. Mr A. Findlay, the national benefactor, impressed upon his visitors on Thursday last the great benefit of using whole seed. He maintained that the extra cost in seed is more than compensated for by a more vigorous plant and a heavier yield of larger potatoes. His view appears to be corroborated by the experience of a potato grower in New Zealand. Mr David Dun of Greenhills, Gore, N.Z., late of Mains of Kilconquhar, Fife, and Baldinnies, Perth, contributes to a New Zealand paper the results of trials he conducted with The Bruce, with the object of throwing light upon this point. The crop throughout was an enormous one, the figures showing a yield at the rate of from 13 tons 12½ cwt. to 21 tons 10 cwt. per acre. The result of the trial was a victory for the uncut seed, although seed with two eyes gave a very large return. As to the size of whole seed, the results show egg-sized to be quite as good as large-sized tubers. With ordinary manuring, the large-sized had the advantage, but with an extra dressing of iron sulphate the egg-sized shone, and gave the tremendous crop of 21¼ tons to the acre.

Potato Propagation.

(From the *Farming World* of 21st October, 1892.)

Fifeshire is a county of peculiar fame. It is distinguished for the multiplicity of its products, as well as for the abundance of a few. It is only within quite a recent period, however, that "The Kingdom" has mounted the ladder of fame in potato propagation. A potato growing county it has always been, and that on a pretty extensive scale. But it has been left to Mr Archibald Findlay, Markinch, to spread its fame as the birthplace of new varieties of tubers. Mr Findlay has, perhaps, done more than any other man living to maintain and advance the potato-growing trade of this country—and foreign countries as well. For many years he has patiently and studiously prosecuted his favourite pursuit. Success, of course, has not at all times dawned upon his efforts. In fact, failures, or rather partial failures, have been not unfrequent. But heated enthusiasm and perseverance have obscured defeat and printed success indelibly before him. An enthusiast of Mr Findlay's calibre refuses to own the presence of stumbling-blocks. Whatever may be the outcome of his attempt, he goes on year after year experimenting and developing seedlings until he has commanded success to reward his exertions.

Mr Findlay's is a most peculiar study. But it is even more useful than it is strange. The amount of time and pains that he devotes to the propagation and production of new sorts of potatoes are surprising beyond all comprehension. When one hears of the universal popularity of The Bruce, and the rapidly rising fame of Her Majesty, Lady Frances, Jeanie Deans, and many other kinds, he inclines to the idea that the propagation of the potato knows no failure. Mr Findlay has quite a different story to relate. If, he says, he meets success once in every forty attempts, he considers himself fortunate. It often costs him more. When the number of really successful crosses Mr Findlay has been fortunate to secure are considered, some idea of the vast amount of work he devotes in the execution of his adopted hobby may be formed.

The Bruce was the first tuber to bring fame to Markinch. This excellent variety, although it is only seven years since it made its *debut* in the market, is already known almost wherever potatoes are grown. In Scotland, England, and Ireland it has attained an enviable position. Many other good sorts have been abandoned to make room for this favourite plant. Not only has The Bruce proved prolific, but it is a good market potato, and above all, a noted disease-resister. Seldom does it contract the dreaded malady. In these depressed times, the value of this desirable quality can hardly be over-estimated. The Bruce, however, is known and cultivated far beyond the British shores. Only the other day we were shown an account of The Bruce's success in New Zealand. A small quantity having been procured some years ago from headquarters at Markinch by a native of Fife at New Zealand, the variety has created a wonderful reputation in the Antipodes. With shrewdness characteristic of the county of his birth, the original recipient of The Bruce kept them rigidly within his own grasp until his stock had reached considerable dimensions. As a result, he reaped a nice, tidy harvest last year. He was disposing of a big crop at £5 a ton, when his envious neighbours could only command 30s or £2 per ton for their crops. Enough has been said of The Bruce—*he* speaks for himself. A few words about his less-known but promising companions will be equally interesting.

On Thursday of last week, Mr Findlay had his annual "Field Day." A party of his earliest and most ardent supporters, including Mr Lawson of Carriston; Mr A. Hutcheson, Dundee; Mr Cunningham, Dalachy; Mr Braid, Abercrombie; Mr Melville, Ballomill; and Messrs Winton, Ardovie, Brechin, paid a visit to the experimental grounds at Markinch on that day. The gardens where the crossing operations begin were inspected, and afterwards an adjournment was made to the fields, where stems of the more advanced varieties were lifted and examined. In the gardens Mr Findlay has at present more than a dozen different sorts under supervision. As yet they boast of no name, but they are all remarkably strong in shaws, and all show a good return when dug up. It was estimated that they yielded at the rate of from 10 to 16 tons per acre, and were of good, profitable size. More is sure to be heard of some of these. Leaving the unchristened seedlings at present, we came to a new variety about ready to fight its way in the market. This sort bears the fashionable title of Up-to-Date, and gives promise of justifying its suggestive name. It is of nice colour, shape, and size, and dug up in large numbers. The company were unanimous in predicting a great future for Up-to-Date. Specimens of the Thane o' Fife and others were shown here.

From the nursery we drove to Mr M'Gregor's farm at Pitillock, where Mr Findlay has a field of eleven acres under crop. The stock in this field comprised Scottish Chief, a very promising youngster, Lady Frances, The Bruce, Her Majesty, Lady Fife, Thane o' Fife, Early Fortune, Jeanie Deans, and No. 3, and some other sorts unnamed. Every one of these pleased the company unanimously. They were all prolific, and of fair size, although the latter quality was not fully brought out, Mr Findlay preferring "seed size" to "market size," and manuring accordingly—all artificials. If anything, the honours lay with Her Majesty and Lady Frances, but Scottish Chief, Lady Fife, and No. 3 were also remarkably good. It should be noted that Mr Findlay plants all his potatoes whole, and strongly advocates this course.

Mr Lawson's finely managed home farm of Carriston was next visited. Here Lady Fife, No. 2, No. 3, Lady Frances, Her Majesty, and The Bruce were seen to advantage. All were good, but Her Majesty and Lady Frances again shone, the former, in particular, eliciting praise. Mr Lawson showed us a stem of each of the above varieties he planted in the garden, giving each three square feet of space. The yield from these was marvellous in size, number, and quality. The Bruce, if anything, led in this contest, with a tremendous return.

A visit was also paid to Mr Fyshe's excellently conducted farm of Treaton, when a similar process of inspection was gone through with equally satisfactory results. The crop here of all kinds is excellent, and, as at the other places inspected, disease is unknown. The company thereafter returned to Markinch, and, after partaking of Mr Findlay's hospitality, and some speechifying, concluded a most enjoyable and instructive day's outing.

Presentation to the Raiser of The Bruce Potato.

(From the *N. B. Agriculturist* of 19th August, 1891.)

On account of the dinner and presentation to Mr Findlay, Markinch, having taken place last week within an hour of our time for going to press, we were only able to give a very short account of the proceedings. We append a few further notes by way of supplementing our short report of last week.

The Chairman, Mr James Hope, East Barns, in making the presentation, said they all knew the superb quality of The Bruce potato as a very heavy cropper and a most successful resister of disease. He could also testify from his own experience, as also could many others round that board, that the newer varieties raised by Mr Findlay, namely, Lady Fife, Lady Frances, Her Majesty, and Jeanie Deans, were likely to rival even The Bruce, not only as heavy croppers, but as disease-resisters. Mr Hope also mentioned that nearly all the potatoes grown on his farms were of the varieties originated by Mr Findlay, and a large part of the seed was supplied by him.

Mr Hope grows annually over 350 acres of potatoes.

Mr Findlay, in returning his sincere thanks for the honour done him, detailed the remarkable way in which The Bruce had, from the first, proved up to the hilt its prominent claims as a heavy cropper, and its all but complete immunity from disease. Referring to the steps that were now being taken by the Royal Agricultural Society of England and the Highland Society of Scotland to test the sulphate of copper treatment as a preventive or cure of disease, he expressed the decided opinion that the proposed lime and sulphate of copper treatment would be of very little avail in combating the ravages of the disease. It might be of some use in the light crops grown on the lands of the much-behind-time farmers, whose sole business in life seemed to be a blind worship of things antiquated, and an eternal grumbling at the results. (Laughter.) But on the robust, heavy haulmed, and densely foliaged varieties, that would always be the favourites of the progressive farmer, and the great source of food supply to the nation, its application would, in his opinion, be of no avail. Fancy the effect of driving a Strawsonizer, or any other "izer," through a field of The Bruce, which a stranger would require to examine closely before he could say how they were drilled. (Laughter.) He was afraid that to such a crop the cure would be about as bad as the disease. He held that the best remedy against the disease was to have potatoes so robust in themselves as to stand in no need of being cured. He might also mention that the heaviest crops of the best quality he had ever grown were grown almost exclusively with artificial manures. When speaking lately at a public dinner at Dundee, he made reference to his belief that the prospects of potato-growers were brightening. He would again now, but more fully, explain the grounds on which that belief was founded. In the first place, the population was steadily increasing, which meant a larger home consumption. In the second, he was very much of opinion that wheat would be dearer in the near future than it had been in the past, which would likely lead to an increased acreage of that crop, and a consequent curtailment of the present potato acreage. Thirdly, the United States, tariff and altogether, seemed to be getting more extensive buyers year by year of British-grown potatoes. For the year 1890 they had from Scotland, 32,365 tons 10 cwts.; from England, 12,325 tons 2 cwts. 2 qrs.; and from Ireland, 3152 tons 19 cwts. 1 qr., which showed a total of 47,843 tons 11 cwts. 3 qrs. He thought those present would agree with him that the outlook might be said to be fairly good. He concluded by thanking them again for their great kindness, and assured them it would never be forgotten by him.

The Chairman said that, with reference to the great destruction of the potato crop by disease in 1846, he had 100 acres that year, and did not get £100 out of the whole crop. On account of the complete failure of the crop that year, he got an abatement of £80 of his rent for that year, and that was the only rent abatement he had ever received in his life. He thought with Mr Findlay that the prospects for British agriculturists were decidedly improving. He could not help thinking also that if the Government were so very anxious to get at the best way of combating the potato disease, they might call a really practical man like Mr Findlay to their councils, as he would be able to give them most valuable assistance in that important matter. He proposed that they dedicate a bumper to the health of Mr Fyshe, the secretary, for the admirable way in which he had managed the whole of the work connected with the testimonial fund. Mr Fyshe was well known to them all, not only as a prominent and enterprising agriculturist, but also as a gentleman who had won the sincere respect of a wide circle of friends and acquaintances. (Applause.)

Mr Fyshe, in responding, said that the credit of getting up this token of appreciation for the services rendered to potato-growers by Mr Findlay really belonged to Mr Hope, though he (the speaker) had done all that he could to forward the movement. He regretted to say, however, that the names of many of those who had benefited most by Mr Findlay's labours had been conspicuous by their absence from the subscription lists. He hoped the potato-growers of the Lothians would support Mr Findlay, who, if he had belonged to many other countries, would have been made a professor long before then. (Laughter.)

The Chairman, in proposing "The Press," said they, as agriculturists, were all greatly indebted to the agricultural press, and he did not know anyone who was doing more to forward the interests of agriculture by his writings than their friend Mr Young of the *N. B. Agriculturist*, with whose name he begged to couple this toast. (Applause.)

Mr Young responded.

In responding to the toast of his health, the croupier, Mr Lawson, Carriston, said The Bruce practically made its *debut* on his farm. He had lately been trying some of the newer varieties introduced by Mr Findlay, and he had been particularly pleased with Her Majesty. In fact, he thought it would even displace The Bruce yet. ("No, no.") Well, he thought so at any rate; and he also thought that Her Majesty was well entitled to be at the top of the trade. (Laughter.) He had lately received a communication from New Zealand, stating that The Bruce was carrying all before it there, and would soon be at the top of the trade in that colony.

A cordial vote of thanks to the Chairman terminated the proceedings.

(From the *Dundee Advertiser* of 13th August, 1891.)

Mr Archibald Findlay, Markinch, was entertained at dinner in the Waterloo Hotel, Edinburgh, this week, by a number of leading agriculturists and others from Fifeshire and other counties in Scotland, and presented with a cheque for upwards of £100 in recognition of his valuable services in the improvement of the potato plant. Mr James Hope of East Barns, Dunbar, presided, and was supported by Mr Archibald Findlay, Markinch; Mr James Fyshe, Treaton; Mr T. Lawson of Carriston, Fife; Mr G. Dun, Kincaple; Mr Smith, Longniddry; Mr Melville, Ballomill; Mr D. Farquhar, Glasgow; Mr Mitchell, Lauriston; Mr Fyshe, Newtonlees; Mr J. Curror, Kirkcaldy; Mr Blyth; Mr Young, Edinburgh; Mr Page, Myregornie, &c. Mr Fyshe, secretary, read letters of apology for absence from Captain Gilmour of Lundin and Montrave; Mr Banks, Grangehill; Mr P. Hunter; Mr Alexander Westwood, sen., Cupar; Mr Hutcheson, Dundee; Mr Stenhouse, Cramond; Mr Bisset, Balfarg; and Mr Steel of Blair.

The Chairman said that, as they were all aware, they had met to do honour to their friend Mr Findlay, and they knew better than he could tell them the very great trouble and expense that that gentleman had been at in raising new varieties of potatoes. If for nothing more than in giving them The Bruce potato, he thought Mr Findlay had done the country a service. He could say for himself that he had benefited very largely by The Bruce potato. But Mr Findlay had also brought out Lady Fife, Her Majesty, and Jeanie Deans, and he could not tell them how many more. He could speak for these varieties being first-rate, and he was sure that a year or two would prove it. While thanking Mr Findlay for what he had done in the past, they still looked forward to him doing a great deal in the future. (Applause.) A year or two ago the Highland Society offered prizes for new varieties of potatoes, but he did not know if their friend was in the field at that time. It was thought then that any variety that was brought forward was scarcely worthy of merit, and the thing was allowed to collapse. He had urged the Society two or three times since to act, but they were very old-fashioned, and liked to conserve their money in a way that some of their members did not approve of. The amount which had been subscribed as a testimonial to Mr Findlay testified to the good feeling of the gentlemen round the table and many others who were not present. (Applause.) He was sure that they wished Mr Findlay great success, as what he had done must have cost him very much trouble and anxiety. He hoped that Mr Findlay would be spared to reap some benefit from a pecuniary point of view, for so far the benefit had all been to those who had used the new varieties. (Hear, hear, and applause.) The Chairman then handed a cheque for upwards of £100 to Mr Findlay, and trusted he would long be spared to benefit the agriculture of this country. (Loud applause.)

Mr Findlay, who was received with applause, thanked all who had subscribed towards the magnificent gift which had just been placed in his hands. It was very gratifying to him to know that his humble efforts had met not only with approval, but had been considered worthy of the honours of that day. It was also very gratifying to him to know that The Bruce potato, like the warrior king whose name it bears, still holds sway in Scotland, and carries on a career of peaceful conquest all over the empire, and he might with equal truth say all over the world wherever potatoes are grown. (Applause.)

The Chairman proposed the health of Mr Fyshe, the secretary, and attributed the success of that meeting and of the testimonial mainly to what that gentleman had done. (Applause.)

Mr Fyshe, in responding, gave the credit to the Chairman, but urged the farmers of the Lothians to support Mr Findlay, who, in his opinion, would have been made a professor in some countries. (Laughter and applause.)

Potato Culture in Fife.

(From the *N. B. Agriculturist* of 7th October, 1891.)

On Friday, a party of farmers and others interested in potato culture paid a visit to Markinch for the purpose of inspecting the well-known trial grounds of Mr Archibald Findlay, the eminent potato raiser of that district. As most of our readers are aware, Mr Findlay has devoted much time and attention to the subject of potatoes and potato culture for several years, and at the present moment he holds a reputation second to none in the country as a raiser of new and valuable varieties. His greatest success has probably been The Bruce, a potato which rapidly attained to the position of a standard variety in most parts of the country; but his name will also be honourably associated with the Lady Fife, Lady Frances, Jeanie Deans, Her Majesty, and other newer varieties which are year by year growing in popular favour and esteem. But though Mr Findlay has thus already attained great and well-deserved success in the enterprise to which he has so ungrudgingly given up his time and talents, he does not intend to retire on his laurels, or to give up the experiments which have been fraught with so much advantage to the farming community. On the contrary, he is as enthusiastic on the subject as ever, and as intent on doing what he can to further the interest of all who have any stake in the potato-producing capabilities of the country. As an indication of this, it may be mentioned that this year Mr Findlay has no fewer than between three and four hundred new varieties under cultivation and observation.

The visitors on Friday arrived at Markinch in the forenoon, and were almost immediately conducted to a series of small plots in the vicinity of the village where the young hybrids are first tried before being planted out on anything like a large scale. The soil of the plots consists for most part of a deep rich loam, which has grown potatoes continuously for the better part of fifty years. It is mostly low lying, and being naturally of a moist nature, is very favourable for potato testing. The varieties seen here were mostly very young sorts, first and second year's growth; but many of them were full of promise, both as to quantity and quality of yield, and disease-resisting capabilities. In only a very few cases was there any marked tendency to disease, the varieties being generally sound and vigorous-like growers. This was all the more noteworthy that the soil in which they were growing was such as might reasonably be expected to produce disease, if such were going. In this connection, it may be worthy of mention that Mr Findlay plants all his seed in the plots, as well as in the open field, in whole potatoes, and does not follow the prevalent custom of cutting. He maintains that a vastly better and more equal crop is got from whole than from cut seed, and certainly this theory received very convincing confirmation in the course of the day. After spending about an hour at the trial plots, the party mounted a brake and drove to Mr Macgregor's farm of Pitillock, about two miles distant, where Mr Findlay was able to show the visitors the results of some of his newer varieties under field cultivation. On the way, a splendid field of The Bruce, on the home farm of Balbirnie, was noted with much interest, and no small amount of admiration. The field was quite one of the best, so far, at least, as appearance went, that had been seen that day, the haulms still retaining their original upright position, and looking comparatively fresh and green. At Pitillock, the varieties inspected included the Jeanie Deans, the Lady Frances, Her Majesty, and one or two others which have not been named. The palm seemed to be awarded to the Jeanie Deans, which was not only proving itself a good disease-resister, but a heavy cropper. It was estimated that this variety would easily lift twelve tons per acre all over. This potato is now in extensive cultivation in many parts of the country, and in Ayrshire, where such a large quantity of early potatoes are grown, it is giving unmixed satisfaction. One of the largest growers in that county has grown it for the past two years, and is more than satisfied with the result, describing the Jeanie Deans as one of the best varieties he has ever seen. The Lady Frances, which was certified at the great root show at Kilmarnock in October last as the best dish of potatoes then exhibited, and Her Majesty, which won the first prize at the same show as the best round potato, and was much admired at the recent International Horticultural Exhibition in Edinburgh, appeared also to be likely to yield a heavy crop of good-sized, sound tubers. A completely new variety planted on Pitillock was found, on lifting a stem or two, to be quite exceptional in the matter of yield—so much so that one of the party jocularly called it the Farmer's Fortune, a name by which it will, in all probability, become known in the future.

The next stoppage was at Carriston, the esteemed owner and occupier of which, Mr Thos. Lawson, is well-known as one of the best farmers in the county. The potatoes were in a field of about twelve acres, to the south-west of the mansion-house, and were also a very heavy crop. At a moderate estimate they will yield at the rate of twelve tons per imperial acre. Close on one-half of the whole area of the field was under The Bruce, which was a very heavy crop, and all sound; the other varieties represented in the remaining part included the Lady Fife, Jeanie Deans, Lady Frances, and Her Majesty varieties, introduced by Mr Findlay; but amongst the varieties mentioned, the Lady Fife seemed to be the greatest favourite, the stems dug up being not only very rich in yield, but the tubers were beautifully formed, and of a splendid size. Her Majesty, Lady Frances, and Jeanie Deans were also showing themselves to be heavy croppers, and capable of producing a potato of splendid quality under the most varying conditions. Of about a dozen totally new varieties of Mr Findlay's rearing, seen in the field at Carriston, the palm was unanimously given to Nos. 2 and 3, which were both raised from the same parentage, and were found to be exceedingly productive and of good quality. This variety is not unlike the Regent in colour and formation, but is hardly so early as that popular old sort. As showing the prolific nature of these two new varieties, it may be mentioned that single potatoes of each were planted in Mr Lawson's garden at the same time as they were planted in the field; and on the stems being dug up on Friday, one of them was found to have no fewer than thirty-nine good-sized tubers at its roots, and the other twenty-seven. The potatoes had been planted whole about two feet apart, but, notwithstanding this, the extraordinary yield, which was the largest that most of the gentlemen present had ever seen, was much remarked upon.

After leaving Carriston, where they were hospitably entertained by Mr and Mrs Lawson, the strangers proceeded to the neighbouring farm of Treaton, which is occupied by Mr Fyshe, the enterprising secretary of the Windygates Agricultural Society. This year Mr Fyshe has some twenty acres under potatoes, about one-half of which is devoted to The Bruce, which seemed to be doing remarkably well on the soft mossy land on which it was growing. The crop was quite as heavy as at Carriston, and the tubers were, if anything, better shaped than at that farm. Amongst the newer varieties here, Lady Frances and Her Majesty were both maintaining their reputation as exceptionally heavy croppers; but, curiously enough, neither could equal, in yield at least, a two-year-old variety named Up-to-Date, which quite surprised the visitors alike at its superiority of quality and prolific tendencies. It was estimated that quite twelve tons per acre would be gathered from the part of the field devoted to this particular variety. It may be mentioned, as showing the value of pedigree in potato raising as in stock-breeding, that Up-to-Date is from the same cross as Nos. 2 and 3 at Carriston, which were also the best of the new varieties on that farm.

After spending a pleasant two hours on Mr Fyshe's admirably managed holding, the party drove back to Markinch, where they were entertained by Mr Findlay to a sumptuous dinner, which included excellent boilings of the famed Jeanie Deans and a new variety which has not yet undergone the ceremony of christening, but was none the less appreciated on that account. Mr Hope, East Barns, who is not only the largest arable farmer in Scotland, but is the largest and most celebrated potato-grower, presided, and in proposing the health of Mr Findlay, said they, as growers of potatoes, were fully aware of and appreciated the great importance of the work in which their host was engaged. They had greatly benefited in the past by his efforts to introduce new and profitable varieties of potatoes, and, from what they had seen that day, the benefit was likely to be at least as great in the future. (Applause.) Mr Findlay having briefly acknowledged the compliment, which was passed with the greatest enthusiasm, the company separated, having, with delightful weather, spent not only an exceedingly instructive, but an exceedingly enjoyable day.

FINDLAY'S UP-татю-DATE.

I am well persuaded that the British agriculturist has now before him in Up-to-Date the finest maincrop kidney-shaped potato ever hitherto placed in his hands. I have for years grown it under the most varied and trying conditions possible, and have always found it HARDY AS THE BRUCE AND QUITE AS PRODUCTIVE, AND WHEN COOKED FIRM AS THE OLD VICTORIA, AND DRY, FLOURY, AND FULL-FLAVOURED AS THE OLD YORKSHIRE REGENT.

Both in haulm and tuber it is quite distinct from any other potato I am acquainted with. The haulm, though strong and upright, is only of medium height, with foliage of bright green colour, while the tubers are generally of a handsome elongated oval shape, with eyes up to the surface, and the skin of the finest netted appearance imaginable.

For Prices, see current Abridged List.

FINDLAY'S FARMER'S GLORY.

This grand maincrop potato resembles The Bruce in so many points that those who are not close and keen observers, I am afraid, will be disposed to say that it is the same potato with a different name. But this much I can say, that it has little relationship to The Bruce in point of direct parentage, and experience will prove that it excels that remarkable potato in all its strongest points—being more robust and later, and is late in forming its tubers, thereby escaping in a great measure in a dry season what is known as "lady-waist" in long-shaped potatoes; and I would advise, for this reason, that this potato never be raised before being thoroughly ripened off in the haulm, as I find the greater growth of tubers takes place after decay of the haulm has set in. It even excels The Bruce in its adaptability to any sort of soil or climate, flourishing exceedingly under almost forbidding conditions; is of finest table quality from October to July; and its cropping powers are unrivalled. We are disposed to think that in this respect it overshadows The Bruce. In Carriston garden the crop was over thirty tons per imperial acre.

For Prices, see current Abridged List.

FINDLAY'S GOODHOPE.

A most magnificent potato, also of The Bruce type. Quite as hardy and as late, but not so heavy a cropper, yet, at the same time, a very heavy cropper compared with most potatoes in ordinary cultivation—under ordinary field culture yielding crops of from nine to eleven tons per imperial acre. But where potatoes *of the very highest order of quality* are wanted, I am confident Goodhope will stand to the front. The tubers are all of a nice uniform size, with fine netted skin, and eyes up to the surface.

For Prices, see current Abridged List.

FINDLAY'S LADY ROSABELLE.

This latest addition to our lady series of potatoes is a beautiful white round, ripening off in early September, and of remarkable distinctness in the matter of haulm and foliage. It is practically disease-resisting; yields, under ordinary field culture, an abundant crop of beautiful round potatoes, with remarkably rough and finely-netted skins. Was awarded *only medal* for new variety at Kilmarnock Root Show in October, 1891, and in point of table quality leaves nothing to desire: to illustrate which, I beg to recount a late incident. I gave a friend a few to cook, which he did, and his satisfaction was so great that I had to bear a scolding for being so prodigal as to give, or to cook for my own use, any new potato of such extraordinary quality.

No longer Stocked.

FINDLAY'S BRITISH QUEEN

Is one of the finest white kidney-shaped mid-season potatoes, of remarkable distinctness, ripening off same time as Jeanie Deans. On light soil I have never seen a diseased tuber; and even this year—and disease has been very prevalent—I have not seen many diseased tubers, though I had them growing on bare, hilly land. Is a most enormous cropper; grand keeper; cooks firm and dry, with nice full flavour; and is well adapted for field or garden culture.

For Prices, see current Abridged List.

FINDLAY'S RUBY QUEEN

Is a flattish purple round of remarkably fine appearance, grows large but never coarse, and is possibly the heaviest cropping early potato in existence, and its table qualities are of the highest order. The following extract from the letter of an Ayrshire gentleman, under date of July 1st, 1893, confirms in every particular my own opinion as to its claim for earliness and quality:—"*Re* Ruby Queen you so kindly sent me—I lifted them a week ago; and I boiled a few, and find, in a word, they are *perfection*, having flavour and dryness combined. I am very proud of them, and congratulate you.

For Prices, see current Abridged List.

FINDLAY'S SNOWDRIFT

Is, in my opinion, *the finest* and *most productive* white round potato—earliness considered—that has ever yet been offered to the grower. Ripens off about ten days earlier than Ruby Queen, and my experience is that it has no superior, either for exhibition or table purposes. Highly recommended for early work.

No longer Stocked.

FINDLAY'S EIGHTYFOLD

Is a pale purple round of remarkable distinctness, both as regards haulm and foliage. Ripens off about ten days later than Ruby Queen. Is an extraordinary cropper; the tubers are handsome, and its table qualities recall to one's mind the Old Red Fortyfold when at its best. This and the preceding two can all be harvested before disease makes its appearance. Highly recommended for field or garden.

No longer Stocked.

FINDLAY'S PINK-EYED RUSSET

Is in most respects a decided advance upon the common Blacksmith—being a heavier cropper, hardier, and I think of better table quality, and distinct by reason of its eyes being purple.

No longer Stocked.

FINDLAY'S CHALLENGE.

One of the most productive second earlies ever grown. Under ordinary cultivation I have grown 30 lbs. of good sound potatoes, all fit for table use, on $9\frac{1}{2}$ feet of a 24-inch drill; while its handsome appearance, combined with table quality *of the very highest order*, is sure to make it one of the most popular potatoes ever introduced. Ripens off fourteen days before Jeanie Deans. Is exceptionally hardy. Highly recommended for field or garden work.

For Prices, see current Abridged List.

FINDLAY'S AURORA.

This beautiful potato is possibly unique, in so far that it represents the famous Scottish Dons of fifty years ago, being a hybrid out of the old Blue Don. Ripens off in September, is fairly hardy, and an immense cropper; is of the finest table quality, and also well adapted for exhibition purposes.

No longer Stocked.

FINDLAY'S CONQUEST.

In offering this potato, I do so with the conviction that it will be found a decided acquisition to early market growers. It is a beautiful white round, with a fine netted skin, *full of quality;* an enormous cropper, much earlier than the Kemp or Red Bog; though not disease-resisting, is fairly hardy.

For Prices, see current Abridged List.

FINDLAY'S EXHIBITOR.

This is possibly, as its name implies, one of the most beautiful kidney-shaped potatoes ever introduced. It is well adapted for field or garden culture. On medium, light, porous soil, where deep cultivation is practised, I have never seen prettier tubers, so nicely shaped, and beautifully white, and at the same time the skin is finely netted, indicating its fine table qualities; and is practically disease-resisting.

No longer Stocked.

FINDLAY'S JEANIE DEANS.

No potato hitherto introduced ever won, in so short a time, the same high place in public favour as Jeanie Deans has done. I only offered it to the public in small quantities in the autumn of 1890 and in the spring of 1891, 1892, 1893, and 1894, and up to the present time I have had more enquiries, and have sold to parties who have bought previously more of this superb potato than ever I did of the world-renowned potato The Bruce at the same season of the year. When offering this magnificent potato for the first time, in the autumn of 1890, I ventured to say that it was, in our opinion, a decided advance on every early potato yet in cultivation, in respect of its great disease-resisting power, heavy cropping, and fine cooking qualities, and that its keeping qualities were quite phenomenal. Notwithstanding that it ripens off in August, it can be kept and will lose little of its fine cooking qualities until past midsummer of the following season.

For Prices, see current Abridged List.

FINDLAY'S EARLY BEAUTY.

This remarkably fine potato may be well described as a later Jeanie Deans. Growing side by side, a casual observer would say they were the same, the colour of foliage and habit of growth being almost identical; but closer examination would reveal that the growth of top was considerably stronger in this variety, and ripens off about ten or fourteen days later than Jeanie Deans; and then the tubers are generally rounder, and the skin very much more netted.

No longer Stocked.

FINDLAY'S LADY FIFE

Is a forward second early, round, and of fairly robust habit of growth. The tubers are numerous, large, and of a flattish round shape, with a beautifully netted skin—eyes few and shallow. Though growing large it never becomes coarse, is a very heavy cropper and well adapted for field culture, and is gradually taking the highest place in the class to which it belongs. Its cooking qualities are of a very high order, and it resists disease in a most remarkable degree.

No longer Stocked.

FINDLAY'S LADY FRANCES.

This grand mid-season Maincrop Potato ripens off early in September, and is as remarkable for its fine cooking and table qualities as for its heavy cropping and *disease-resisting powers.* The haulm is strong and upright, and though well adapted for garden work, if room is given, is one of the most vigorous and beautiful potatoes under ordinary field culture that is before the agriculturist.

For Prices, see current Abridged List.

FINDLAY'S HER MAJESTY

Is one of the most beautiful, yet robust and heavy cropping maincrop potatoes in cultivation, and has yielded under ordinary field culture at the rate of from twelve to twenty tons per imperial acre. The tubers are round, with few and flat eyes, and finely netted skin. Generally large, but never becoming coarse, they are as well adapted for the exhibition table as the majority that are ever shown, thus combining fine form with general utility; while the vigour of the plant enables it to withstand disease in a very high degree—in fact, few potatoes have greater disease-resisting power. As a table potato it has few equals. In our estimation, this potato has a great future. As an exhibition variety it has taken leading honours wherever shown, and was awarded First Prize at the great Root Show held at Kilmarnock on 23rd October, 1890, as the best round, in competition with all the best rounds in cultivation.

No longer Stocked.

FINDLAY'S THE BRUCE.

This world-renowned potato still maintains its place as the best kidney-shaped maincrop potato in commerce.

CAUTION.—Many potatoes have, I am led to believe, been sold as The Bruce or Bruce's that never at any time came from me, and are consequently not true stock. This caution, I am sorry to say, also applies to most of my other introductions.

(From the *North British Agriculturist* of 21st October, 1891.)

THE BRUCE POTATO IN NEW ZEALAND.—The Bruce, which is now so largely cultivated at home, has found its way to the Antipodes, where so many of its countrymen have found a prosperous and congenial home. Writing the other day from Greenhill, Gore, New Zealand, to a friend in the home (Fife) of this new celebrated tuber, Mr David Dun, formerly of Baldinnes, in Perthshire, and subsequently of Kilconquhar Mains, Fife, says:—The Bruce is likely to do well out here. The few I have just lifted are the produce of 4 lbs. I got from Mr Walker, per parcel post, lifted by him in August, and planted by me in October, 1889, and finer stuff I have never seen north or south of the Line. I am resolved that in Southland they shall be the potato of the future, and am quietly (if that is the word) keeping my doings with them before the public, through notes in the local papers, and exhibition of the tubers at the shows in the district. I mean to get to the top of the seed market in this district by and by, but can't very well till I have another crop secured, the extent of which will be an acre and a half. I am giving The Bruce a chance that few can do, as they are being grown on new land that has never seen a turnip or a potato, and has produced only one crop of oats of over fifty-five bushels per imperial acre. There is plenty of vegetable matter, but just little enough silica perhaps. Such a thing as artificial manure we never dream of here, and I have, as near as I can calculate, some fifteen tons an acre. At one hundred miles from Dunedin, and fifty miles from Bluff, there is no use cultivating potatoes but for the local market, and that is easily overstocked, but The Bruce will make a road for itself.

(From the *Glasgow Herald* of 20th May, 1891.)

The Bruce has been by far the most profitable potato of the season. Unfortunately, however, as often happens under such circumstances, but few farmers in this district grew any. Those who did have every reason to be thankful, and many consider themselves specially fortunate.

(From the *Liverpool Weekly Mercury* of 27th February, 1892.)

The Bruce Potato.—"Topsham" (Exeter).—You are quite right in making inquiries respecting this potato, as I believe it is a kind that would do well in your district, as, indeed, it does everywhere. It has not been in commerce many years, and originated in Scotland. There is rather too much top growth to it to be suitable for a small garden, but as a field sort it is excellent, and not only verifies its name of being disease-resisting, but it is prolific and first-rate in quality. Like yourself, I would not be disposed to give 3s 6d per 14 lbs. for seed, as it may be bought at 6s or 7s per cwt., or probably a little more for selected tubers. Be sure you secure the right sorts—true to name.

(From the *Mataura Ensign* (N.Z.) of 25th March, 1892.)

R. A. B. communicates to the *New Zealand Farmer* the following results of this season's crop of the above-named famous variety of potato (The Bruce), and it forms a most useful contribution to the question of planting whole or cut sets. The extent of each plot was exactly the same, the land was in good condition, and the manure used was artificial. No special care was taken to pick the primest seed, the usual care being taken to choose good seed and nothing more.

Size of Seed Used.	Cwt.	Qr.	Lb.
A			
*1. Alley-taw size, picked from refuse seed, 8 inches apart	14	1	14
2. Small seed from general crop, planted whole	11	3	14
3. Small seed, late planted and starved, planted whole	10	2	14
B			
4. Egg-size seed, seed ends cut off, weighed before cutting off	22	2	0
5. Egg-size, cut into two lengthwise	11	3	14
6. Egg-size, cut into pieces with two eyes each	10	0	0
7. Egg-size, planted whole	21	1	20
†8. Egg-size, planted whole, and extra manured with iron sulphate	25	0	0
C			
9. Large-size potatoes, cut into pieces with one eye each	13	3	0
10. Large-size, cut into halves, lengthwise	28	3	0
11. Large-size, all eyes bar one cut out and the wounds limed	61	1	0
12. Large-size, planted whole	51	3	14
13. Large-size, planted whole	55	0	0
†14. Large size, planted whole, and extra manured with iron sulphate	44	1	14

* The only row planted at this distance; all others at 1 ft. apart.
† One pound of sulphate of iron to each row.

The "spuds" were dug up, sorted and weighed on the 13th February with the following results:—

No.	Lbs.	Large.	Small.		Per Acre Tons.	Cwt.
1	115	80 lbs.	35 lbs.	at the rate of	14	7½
2	109	85 lbs.	24 lbs.	,, ,,	13	12½
3	123	98 lbs.	25 lbs.	,, ,,	15	7½
4	113	81 lbs.	32 lbs.	,, ,,	14	2½
5	114	95 lbs.	19 lbs.	,, ,,	14	5
6	130	115 lbs.	15 lbs.	,, ,,	16	5
7	149	122 lbs.	27 lbs.	,, ,,	18	12½
8	172	133 lbs.	39 lbs.	,, ,,	21	10
9	125	95 lbs.	30 lbs.	,, ,,	15	12½
10	136	106 lbs.	30 lbs.	,, ,,	17	0
11	166	132 lbs.	34 lbs.	,, ,,	20	15
12	144	90 lbs.	54 lbs.	,, ,,	18	0
13	164	112 lbs.	52 lbs.	,, ,,	20	10
14	167	100 lbs.	67 lbs.	,, ,,	20	17½

The crop itself all through the plot was splendid for sample. I have never seen a yield so handsome, shapely, and true to type. There were not twenty potatoes away from their proper form. As far as yield goes, I have authenticated accounts of bigger crops, but this has not been a record season for us in North New Zealand. Only one row out of the fourteen, it may be noticed, turned out less than at the rate of 14 tons per acre. The highest was 21½ tons. The average for the plot was over 17 tons per acre, or, as a man said who threw a stone at his dog, but hit his mother-in-law, "Not so bad."

LATEST INTRODUCTIONS.

GRAND NEW HYBRID POTATO,

FINDLAY'S LANGHOLME MODEL,

Second Early White Kidney.

In all my long experience I have never seen a more handsome potato than this. A free grower, a big cropper, of exceptional cooking quality, and wonderfully hardy for a potato ripening off at about the same time as British Queen. A sure seller as a commercial potato, and a certain prizetaker on the exhibition table. Altogether a potato we always wish to but seldom see.

GRAND NEW HYBRID POTATO,

FINDLAY'S MAIRSLAND QUEEN,

White Round, Forward Second Early.

I beg again to submit to your notice what I believe is one of the most productive and hardy early potatoes it has been my good fortune to raise, and in corroboration of this would relate a circumstance that occurred in the beginning of September of 1904. I had a party of five of the leading potato experts at Mairsland making a tour of inspection; on digging a root of this I jocularly asked if the tubers were worth £20 each. To my surprise, first one, then another bought, until all the company had one at this price.

GRAND NEW EARLY HYBRID POTATO,

FINDLAY'S GOLD REEF.

It gives me much pleasure to introduce to your notice a potato of such sterling worth. I shall be much disappointed if it does not prove a veritable reef of gold to the grower of early varieties. It is of fairly vigorous habit for an early variety, with foliage of a distinctly golden tinge; a big cropper of beautiful white kidney-shaped tubers, of finest cooking quality.

GRAND NEW FORWARD SECOND EARLY POTATO,

FINDLAY'S DIAMOND REEF,

White Kidney.

I esteem it a special good fortune that I am able to offer at this time such an exceptionally grand potato as this. It is so forward as almost to rank as a first early. It is a big cropper; the tubers leave nothing to desire in the matter of fine appearance; the cooking qualities are of the highest order. It is wonderfully robust, and hardy beyond anything I have known, ripening off so early. In my estimation an ideal potato with an assured future.

GRAND NEW MID-SEASON POTATO,

FINDLAY'S MILLION MAKER.

This is decidedly one of the most distinct mid-season potatoes I have ever known, and one of the hardiest. I have not yet seen one tuber affected with disease, notwithstanding the disastrous years we have passed through since it was raised six years ago. The bloom is white, the haulm and foliage of a pale green colour, of fair vigour, giving plenty of cover. The tubers are, in all my experience, of the finest kidney shape I have ever seen, while the cooking quality is superb.

FINDLAY'S ELDORADO,

New Mid-Season White Elongated Oval Disease-Resisting Potato.

This potato is one of the most prolific and disease-resisting which it has been my good fortune to offer. In character of stem and foliage it much resembles Royal Kidney, but it is more robust in habit, and the foliage is of a darker green. The tubers, though generally more elongated and kidney-shaped, show in a general way a good deal of the type of Evergood. The bloom, however, is very much like that of Goodfellow. It is with me a fairly free bloomer, while neither Evergood nor Royal Kidney bloom at all. Goodfellow does bloom, but only in a meagre way. That it has in some parts a resemblance to all those three will be no great wonder when you know the strain in it is the same.

GRAND NEW MAINCROP POTATO,

FINDLAY'S GREAT SCOT,

Disease-Resisting.

I think I can now claim to have raised and introduced to your notice a few potatoes that have made their way to fame by sterling merit. I again offer you in the Great Scot another aspirant to a place on the highest pinnacle.

In the first place, no potato is more immune from attacks of blight. The haulm is vigorous, giving grand cover. The tubers are ovate round, with a slight trace of pale pink in the eyes. The crop is most abundant. As a cooker it is one of the best.

FINDLAY'S NORTHERN STAR,

White Round, Late,

NEW (1902) DISEASE-RESISTING POTATO.

In my career as a raiser of new varieties of potatoes, I think it will be generally conceded that I have introduced a few that have made a reputation. But of all I have sent out, not one of them so nearly approaches my ideal potato as this. It is a heavy cropper, of fine shape and quality, and the most disease-resisting and weather-defying potato I have ever known.

FINDLAY'S ROYAL KIDNEY,

White Kidney,

NEW (1901) DISEASE-RESISTING POTATO.

I am now for the sixth time offering this grand potato. I offer it as one of the hardiest I have ever sent out—never having yet seen a tuber affected with disease during all the years I have grown it; and I think it would be hardly possible to have more trying seasons than 1899 and 1900. As a cropper it will be difficult to surpass, or to find a potato with a finer appearance, while its table qualities will be found of the highest order—firm, dry, and of fine flavour. In habit of growth it is fairly strong, giving nice cover. It ripens off third week of September, and is a grand keeper.

FINDLAY'S GOODFELLOW,

White Round,

NEW (1901) DISEASE-RESISTING POTATO.

Now offered for the sixth time, is of vigorous habit of growth, and exceptionally hardy; an enormous cropper of even-sized tubers of finest table quality, and a grandkeeper. To those who prefer round potatoes this will be found a great acquisition. It responds exceptionally well to high cultivation. Recommended as well worthy of attention.

FINDLAY'S COLONIST,

Pink Round,

NEW (1901) DISEASE-RESISTING POTATO.

Our colonies seem to prefer coloured potatoes, hence the name; but at the same time many potatoes with more colour have been great favourites in the home market. The colour of this one is so slight that I have no doubt of its making headway at home by reason of its many good qualities. It is an enormous cropper, practically free from disease, even in this bad year. As a table potato it has few equals. Excepting Up-to-Date, I know of no potato so easily grown.

FINDLAY'S EVERGOOD,

NEW MID-SEASON DISEASE-RESISTING POTATO.

In offering this potato for the seventh season, I am confident that it will in every way bear out that it has got an appropriate name—being of first-class cooking quality, admitting of it taking its place as a forward mid-season early; is of nice plump oval shape, with a fine white clean skin; a heavy cropper of equal sized tubers. In the years I have had it under observation I have not seen a diseased tuber.

FINDLAY'S MR AMBROSE,

Pink Round,

NEW (1901) EARLY POTATO.

This is one of the nicest early potatoes I have met with. In colour, pale pink; in shape, a true round, with very few and flat eyes. An enormous cropper; of fine table quality; sure to be popular when known, especially in the Colonies.

FINDLAY'S HIBERNIA,

Pink Round,

NEW (1901) LATE, DISEASE-RESISTING POTATO.

Hardy, vigorous, big cropper, of fine table quality; sure to be a favourite in the Colonies and in Ireland.

FINDLAY'S NEW EMPRESS QUEEN,

A New Selection of exceptional merit,

LATE OR MAINCROP DISEASE-RESISTING POTATO.

This I now offer for the third time, and say without hesitation that I am satisfied this potato will be more popular than my first. I think it superior to this potato in all that has gone to make it so popular, and that in point of quality and shape it has some advantages. In point of cooking I have seen few potatoes that surpass it. It is of a nice kidney shape, giving a bold and taking sample. I anticipate a great future for this potato.

FINDLAY'S QUEEN OF THE VELDT,
NEW MID-SEASON PURPLE KIDNEY,
Disease-Resisting.

After years of careful growing—it being our favourite for home use—I now offer this potato for the third time, in the full conviction that there is no potato of its class with so many points to recommend it to the cultivator. Its cooking quality is exceptional; it has done well in all kinds of soil, is a great cropper, an exceptional free grower, grand keeper, and remarkably hardy. I anticipate it will hold the position I have assigned it in South Africa.

GRAND NEW EARLY HYBRID POTATO,
FINDLAY'S KLONDYKE,
Field of Gold,
A New Selection of Great Merit.

In bringing this potato under the notice of those who make the growing of potatoes for the early market a speciality, I am convinced there has never been offered before a potato in this class combining so many good qualities. In habit of growth it is as vigorous as many second earlies, while in point of cropping I have seen few of this class equal to it. I have dug as many as 6¼ pounds to a root; in fact, on the whole, it yields enormously, and the quality, when cooked, is far above the average of its class; yet I have had it on my table two months from date of planting—that is as from 1st May to 1st July. Boxing is recommended for this potato, and change of seed from year to year.

GRAND NEW MID-SEASON POTATO,
FINDLAY'S BRITISH QUEEN, No. 2,
White Ovate Round Forward Second Early.

This potato in general appearance so much resembles one of its parents—my popular British Queen—that I have not seen my way to give it more distinction than by naming it British Queen, No. 2. It has all the good qualities of the first, with the advantage of being earlier. Has less top, does not bloom so freely, and with me less liable to disease. Its cooking qualities are of the highest order, while as a cropper it has few equals.

GRAND NEW MAINCROP POTATO,

FINDLAY'S UP-TO-DATE, No. 2,

White Ovate Round.

This potato has so many features in common with the original Up-to-Date that the description of the old will do for the new—with this exception, that I think it has fully more top, and the cooking quality is of a superior order.

FINDLAY'S EMPIRE KIDNEY,

New Disease-Resisting Potato.

This fine potato is of The Bruce type—not quite so strong in the haulm, but strong enough to give ample cover; produces a heavy crop of beautiful even tubers of grand quality. Has with me given best results on fertile loam, and will be a favourite with growers cultivating this class of land, and in our leading markets.

The Outlook for Potatoes.

A VISIT TO Mr A. FINDLAY, AT LANGHOLME MANOR, HAXEY, LINCOLNSHIRE.

Mr Findlay has obeyed the instincts of his race. He has turned his face South. Not content with being a Scottish laird in one of the hilliest and most delightful parts of Fifeshire, he has within the last few months become an English landowner in one of the flattest and least interesting parts of Lincolnshire. He thinks that his customers will be the gainers by what I cannot help describing as an act of self-sacrifice. For who, in the pursuit of his own pleasure, would exchange the lovely views over the Lomonds of Fife, which Mr Findlay commands from his home at Mairsland, for the dreary landscapes of the Isle of Axholme?

There is this to be said about the prospect from Langholme Manor, Mr Findlay's new home. It embraces another county. But this cannot very well be avoided, seeing that when you have crossed the road opposite Mr Findlay's house, you have left Lincolnshire and entered Nottinghamshire.

Mr Findlay came to settle in Lincolnshire in this wise. He was staying a little time ago with Mr Blaydes, the well-known potato-grower of Epworth, and as they were driving to the station Mr Blaydes pointed out to him Langholme Manor, an estate of 420 acres, which was for sale. He said to Mr Findlay, "Why don't you buy it?" and he expatiated on the manifold advantages of the situation. "Here," said he, "is warp-land, some of the finest soil in the whole world for potatoes; here is a railway station—Haxey—right in the middle of the estate; and look how conveniently for farming operations the fields are arranged. The high road runs alongside them for two miles." Thus—and more—quoth the eloquent Mr Blaydes, and Mr Findlay, knowing a good thing when he sees it, could not deny that, in the words of his favourite Scottish poet, it looked a "cosie place." So, within a comparatively short space, the title deeds of Langholme Manor changed hands, and Mr Findlay became domiciled in England.

When I visited him there last week one of my first questions related to his old home, of which I possess pleasant memories. Did he not yearn for his native heather? Sentiment seemed to demand that he should say "Yes." But he said "No." He had never enjoyed better health in his life, he told me, than since coming to the Isle of Axholme, and although he should, of course, return from time to time to Mairsland, yet he thought Langholme would henceforth become his headquarters. And his son Andrew seconded him in these unpatriotic views! He also has found the air of Lincolnshire even more exhilarating than the air on the hillsides of Fife. But there is another son, Frank, who "stands by" the old home at Mairsland, and who manages in his father's absence the extensive potato-growing business in the North.

Nobody's views on potatoes are of more general interest than Mr Findlay's, and especially is this the case at the beginning of September, when uncertainty prevails as to what the season will bring forth. His total acreage of potatoes, both in England and Scotland, is 300. The condition of the potato crop in Scotland is, he says, perfection. In Lincolnshire the crop is not quite so good. Taking the Scotch crop at 100, he would approximate the Lincolnshire crop at 85. On his own farm at Haxey the potatoes look "grand," but to some of the crops in the same district this adjective certainly cannot be applied. Mr Findlay does not think that it will be an exceptional year for yields. It may, indeed, be under the average. But as many of the varieties do most of their work during the present month, it is almost impossible at this stage to speak positively on the subject.

Although he has been established at Langholme only since February, Mr Findlay told me that he had learnt a very great deal about the trying conditions under which the English growers pursue their business. "The English climate," to use his own expression, "punishes the potato fearfully." At the same time he thinks that it is possible, by a knowledge of the best conditions of growing, to circumvent this enemy. He has already come to the opinion, however, that Scotland is much more of an ideal place for potatoes than England, not excepting the favoured district of the Isle of Axholme.

I was naturally curious to hear his views as to the trade outlook. Last season, he said, was a very bad one, but he had expected it would be. "There was bound," he remarked, "to be a backwash from the high prices of the previous year." He is cheerful about the outlook for the present season. "The prospect for a good potato is," he stated, "as bright as ever it was."

There is no need for Mr Findlay to assure the agricultural public that he has a number of "really good potatoes." The agricultural public has been aware of that fact for many years past. But what they want to know is if his price for them will be high or low.

A question as to his policy in this matter elicited the following reply: "I mean to put my older varieties upon the market this season at popular prices. My leading lines will be Up-to-Date No. 2, Northern Star, Evergood, and Royal Kidney."

"And what about your highly-priced new varieties?"

"Mairsland Queen, of which I sold a fair quantity last year at £20 to £25 a tuber, will this year be £25 a pound. Gold Reef will be £2 10s a pound, Million Maker £2 10s, and Great Scot £2."

"Are you introducing any new varieties?"

"Only one—Langholme Model. The price of that will be £25 a tuber. It is the prettiest kidney-shaped potato I have ever seen. I have only a very limited quantity. It is a late mid-season potato."

"How about Eldorado?"

"My price for that will be 10s a pound. I still hold the same opinion I have always held about it, that it is one of the very best potatoes ever introduced. There is not a hardier potato in existence, nor a better cropper. But it has not had a fair chance. There has been more cold water thrown upon Eldorado already than has drowned twenty potatoes, but I have no hesitation in saying that it will be one of the popular potatoes of the future. It was just the same when I introduced Up-to-Date. In fact, every one of my most popular potatoes has undergone the same amount of opposition."

The story of the Eldorado boom is now ancient potato history, but Mr Findlay told me once again how opposed he had been to it, and how he had used his most strenuous efforts to discourage it. "I set my back against it all through," he observed, "and got myself into a good deal of odium with all my friends because I did so, whereas in reality I was the only friend they had. I held it back until I had it thoroughly purified and fit to place on the market, and until I had it in a large enough quantity to deal with at a reasonable price." And he added with emphasis: "It would have been eternal ruin to me—not financially, for I could have lined my pockets with money over and over again—but to my reputation, if I had acted in any other way. I had an offer of £200,000 for my stock of Eldorados, but of course I refused it."

It is Mr Findlay's intention to bring fresh potato seed from Scotland every year for planting at Langholme. Buyers will, therefore, have the option either of Scotch seed, or of seed grown one year on the Lincolnshire land. As I have already stated, Langholme is mostly warp land. Potatoes from this class of land have, as most farmers know, a high character for seed.

Of Mr Findlay's general farming operations I may say that he has just completed a most successful corn harvest, and has one of the best-filled stackyards I have seen for some time. He estimates his wheat at six quarters to the acre, and his crop of oats (the Up-to-Date, his own introduction, which he describes as "the oat of the future") was, he said, "a sight." All his farming stock, both live and dead, he brought with him from Scotland—the cost of removal was £400—and his two-wheeled harvest carts and lively Clydesdale horses have made the natives of Haxey open their eyes. Mr Findlay's twelve Clydesdales are certainly splendid animals. One of their chief merits in his eyes is that "they never seem to think that they have time to walk." For their benefit he is building new stables. But building operations are in progress everywhere. The old Manor House is being renovated from ground-floor to attic, a stately wall is being erected in front of it, and the farm buildings are all in a state of transition.

Close to the house an experimental garden is being planned, a new orchard will soon be planted, and, more important still, a new water supply is shortly to be tapped. The hand of the new master of Langholme is indeed to be seen at every turn, and, apart from potatoes, there is more than enough to keep even the most active man from getting "rusty."

There is one thing that Mr Findlay specially desired me to mention to the readers of this paper. It is a word of welcome. "Tell them," he said, "to come and see my crops for themselves. Those three large fields of Northern Stars, side by side—you remember them—I wish everybody who takes an interest in potatoes would come and see what they look like. I don't think they could possibly look better. Lincolnshire isn't Scotland. It's so easy to reach. And Langholme is close to Haxey station."

This is Mr Findlay's invitation card. I don't think anything need be added to it, except the four letters—R. S. V. P.

W. C. SAMBROOK.

Mr A. Findlay in Lincolnshire.

Noted Scotch Potato Grower's Farm at Haxey.

His Views on Eldorados.

(From *The Lincolnshire, Boston, and Spalding Free Press* of 5th September, 1905.)

Some time ago we announced that Mr Archibald Findlay, of Mairsland, Auchtermuchty, N.B., had purchased Langholme Manor Farm, Haxey, Lincolnshire, between Gainsborough and Doncaster, with the idea of using it chiefly in connection with his seed potato growing business, and placing himself in more direct contact with the English grower. Last week, a representative of this journal paid a visit to Haxey, and was conducted by Mr Findlay and his son, Mr Andrew Findlay, over the farm, which covers an area of 420 acres, is within easy distance of the station, and is bounded the full length by a good public road. It should be mentioned that while Mr Findlay has taken up his residence on the farm, he still retains Mairsland, which is now in charge of his son, Mr Frank Findlay.

Mr Findlay took possession in February last, and in the few months which have elapsed since that time has demonstrated to his Lincolnshire neighbours that he is a practical farmer, and a man of ideas; indeed, he has considerably surprised some of them. At present about 180 acres are devoted to potatoes, and the rest to general crops, and Mr Findlay is farming in a manner which shows that he means business. Naturally, the methods and ideas in vogue across the Border have not been wholly discarded. The nine pairs of horses at work on the farm are nearly all Clydesdales, brought from Mairsland. Both Mr Findlay and his son swear by them, considering that they possess more intelligence, more spirit, and more energy than the Shire. This sounds almost like rank heresy in a shire breeding county like Lincoln—but there it is. On the other hand, Mr Findlay brought no men with him, and found no difficulty with local labour. He describes the Lincolnshire labourers as he finds them—"sensible, steady fellows, willing to learn"—the latter quality a necessity with an enterprising man like Mr Findlay. Considerations of space prevent us from more than passing mention of Mr Findlay's building schemes, of which he is his own architect, and which will transform the landscape round the farmhouse. We must get on to the all-important subject—

THE POTATOES.

A tour of inspection showed that there was not an indifferent lot among the whole 180 acres, in spite of the fact that in many cases, owing to the time at which Mr Findlay took over the farm, the tubers were planted somewhat late. Including the Mairsland farm, and the seed put out, Mr Findlay has about 500 acres under potatoes this year. At Langholme there are about 40 acres of Northern Stars, and grand crops they are, too—healthy, vigorous, and level-standing. Eldorados, of which there are several acres, are ripening well, and should produce some excellent seed. Royal Kidneys, which are a favourite with Mr Findlay, are a flourishing lot, as are also the lot of Up-to-Dates. "A grand potato. It will die hard," remarked our guide. British Queens and Evergoods were in no way below the standard. Then there are the plots of unnamed seedlings, which make a gratifying show, and ought to produce something worthy of a christening ceremony. Amongst the newcomers, there are representatives of the Million Maker, Gold Reef, Mairsland Queen—which made £20 to £25 a tuber last year—and a few hybrids.

At the conclusion of our inspection of the farm, Mr Findlay was asked whether the potato boom was over. His reply was :—

"The genuine good potato will always command attention. The prospect for a really good potato is as bright as ever it was."

"The season has hardly started yet, but if we are to judge the main crop portion of the crop from the reports I am getting from the North, it will be a full average crop. You have suffered in the South from climatic conditions. Up to this time I have no reports of blight from Scotland."

THE NEW SEASON'S PRICES.

Asked as to seed prices for the season which is just opening, Mr Findlay said :—

"The prices of my leading things will be moderate. I mean to put the older varieties, like Dates, Stars, Evergoods, Royal Kidneys, &c., upon the market this year at popular prices. My catalogue will be published in the course of a few days."

"For Mairsland Queen, which was selling at £20 to £25 a tuber last year, we still want £25 a pound this year."

"Langholme Model we are offering at £25 a tuber. This will be its first season. It was grown last year as a seedling. It is a long, nice-shaped kidney, with a roughish skin. I think it is, without exception, the prettiest kidney potato I have seen. It is a latish mid-season. This, I may say, is the only thing we are really introducing for the first time this year."

As giving some idea of the work and care entailed in introducing a new variety, it may be stated that the Langholme Model has taken seven years to produce.

A few of the other higher priced varieties will be :—Diamond Reef and Million Maker, £2 10s per lb.; and Great Scot, £2 per lb. Eldorado is priced at 10s per lb., Northern Star at £1 cwt., Klondyke £1 cwt., and British Queen No. 2 £3 cwt. Up-to-Date No. 2, Mr Andrew Findlay said, would grow a beautiful sample on any land, and he had never seen any rough ones among them.

Mr Findlay is now able to give Southern growers the option of having seed grown one year on the Lincolnshire land. It is his intention to bring his seed fresh from Scotland every year. The land at Langholme is mostly what is known as warp land. The potatoes which we had just viewed, he added, had, with slight exception, all been grown with artificial manure, in the following proportion :—Kainit, 3 cwt.; Dewsbury mixture, 10 cwt. The result shows that no great mistake has been made.

THE FUTURE OF ELDORADOS.

Conversation having turned on seasons, Mr Findlay remarked—"Last season was about the worst year in my experience. 1903 was a gentleman to it."

This recalled to his mind the uphill struggle he had in 1893-4-5 with the introduction of the Up-to-Date. "I lost hundreds of pounds over Up-to-Dates those years. No potato has ever cost me so much money to introduce as Up-to-Date. It had to meet a great amount of prejudice and obstruction."

"What about Eldorado?" was the next query.

"I still think it is one of the very best potatoes that ever was. There is no hardier potato in existence. There is no better cropper."

"Do you think growers are going to take it up?"

"There has been more cold water thrown on Eldorado than would have drowned twenty potatoes. At the same time, I have no hesitation in saying that it will be one of the popular potatoes. It has never had a fair chance.

"In the first place, those who had it first dealt with it like fools. They did their level best to sap its constitution by cutting it to pieces, to shreds; and then they were not satisfied with that method of destruction: they had to begin to grow it from shoots. They were dealing with it as an exotic—growing it under glass and with all the forcing methods that their ingenuity or their minds could devise, irrespective of any evil that might follow from it. The next man was never considered. It was wholly done for the selfish purpose of making money out of a popular article.

"I set my back against it, and got myself into a good deal of odium with all my friends. Still, in reality, I was the only friend they had. I held it back until I got it thoroughly purified and in a condition to face the market, and until I had such a quantity to sell, and at such a price, that they would not require to deal with it as these early people had done."

Whilst the Eldorado boom was on, Mr Findlay was offered a fabulous price for his stock, but he refused to line his pockets at the expense of his reputation. To the hundreds of small people who wrote to him at that time for ten, fifty, or a hundred pounds' worth of Eldorado seed, his advice was, "wait until next year." Some of them have wished a good many times since that they had taken that advice.

FINDLAY'S "ROYAL KIDNEY."

FINDLAY'S "MAIRSLAND QUEEN."

FINDLAY'S "EVERGOOD."

FINDLAY'S "NORTHERN STAR."

FINDLAY'S LADY FRANCES

FINDLAY'S JEANIE DEANS

FINDLAY'S HER MAJESTY

FINDLAY'S EARLY BEAUTY

FINDLAY'S SNOWDRIFT

FINDLAY'S RUBY QUEEN

FINDLAY'S LADY FIFE

FINDLAY'S CHALLENGE POTATO

FINDLAY'S "LANGHOLME MODEL."

FINDLAY'S "EMPIRE KIDNEY."

FINDLAY'S "FARMER'S GLORY."

FINDLAY'S "THE BRUCE."

PLOT OF UN-NAMED HYBRID SEEDLINGS.

FINDLAY'S "EMPIRE KIDNEY."

Plot of "Million Maker." Ninety-six Un-named Seedlings in the same Field.

Plot of "Eldorado."

FINDLAY'S "MILLION MAKER."

FINDLAY'S "GREAT SCOTT."

FINDLAY'S "DIAMOND REEF."

FINDLAY'S "GOLD REEF."

Plot of Findlay's "Great Scott."

Plot of Findlay's "Diamond Reef."

Mairsland House (Mr. Findlay's Scottish Residence), nr. Auchtermuchty, Scotland.

Field of Findlay's "Northern Star."

FINDLAY'S "GOLD REEF" (as dug).

FINDLAY'S "DIAMOND REEF" (as dug, with earth adhering).

FINDLAY'S "MAIRSLAND QUEEN" (as dug, earth adhering).

FINDLAY'S "MILLION MAKER" (as dug, with earth adhering).

FINDLAY'S "BRITISH QUEEN II."

FINDLAY'S "MILLION MAKER."

CUP PRESENTED TO THE NATIONAL POTATO SOCIETY BY MESSRS. CARTER & CO., LONDON, AND MR. A. FINDLAY.

READY TO START FOR LANGHOLME.

CARTS FOR LANGHOLME.—MR. FINDLAY'S LINCOLNSHIRE PLACE—IN FRONT OF BUILDER'S PREMISES AT FREUCHIE, FIFE.

LANGHOLME HOUSE FROM PUBLIC ROAD.

LANGHOLME HOMESTEAD FROM PUBLIC ROAD.

Langholme House
from the Lawn
Mr Findlay's
Lincolnshire Residence.

Mairsland House and Steading from the North.

Twenty-month Old Bullock Bred and Fed on Mairsland. Weight 11½ cwt.

Interior View of Findlay's Seed Potato Stores, Auchtermuchty, showing Potatoes in Boxes and Method of Arrangement.

INTERIOR OF FINDLAY'S SEED POTATO STORES, AUCHTERMUCHTY.

Field on Mairsland showing "Eldorado" in the Foreground and Ninety five New Varieties under Test.

West End View of Findlay's Seed Potato Warehouse and Store, Auchtermuchty, N.B.

Printed in Great Britain
by Amazon